EGYPT AND ISRAEL

BY

W. M. FLINDERS PETRIE
D.C.L., LL.D., F.R.S., F.B.A.

PUBLISHED UNDER THE DIRECTION OF THE TRACT COMMITTEE

ISBN: 978-1-63923-693-0

All Rights reserved. No part of this book maybe reproduced without written permission from the publishers, except by a reviewer who may quote brief passages in a review to be printed in a newspaper or magazine.

Printed: February 2023

Published and Distributed By:
Lushena Books
607 Country Club Drive, Unit E
Bensenville, IL 60106
www.lushenabks.com

ISBN: 978-1-63923-693-0

FIG. 2 —"The Prince of the Desert Absha," with an ibex, and his Syrian followers in coats of many colours; the forerunners of the Hyksos migration. They are armed with spears, bows, and throwsticks, carrying a water-skin slung on the shoulders, and playing on a lyre. Beni Hasan, XII Dynasty.

FIG. 3.—Bedawy tent. A mere roof with some stalks round it on the windward side. In Syria, flaps of camel-hair cloth are hung to windward. (p. 14.)

Frontispiece.

NOTICE BY THE TRACT COMMITTEE

THIS work, although it does not altogether represent traditional opinions in regard to the Old and New Testaments, is published as expressing the views of a writer who has done more perhaps than any other to throw light upon the Sacred Writings by his excavations in Bible Lands.

PREFACE

SO many books have appeared dealing with the historical view of the Bible, and treating it in every stage of knowledge, of belief, and of disbelief, that any fresh work of such a scope should state its general line of treatment, and the public for whom it is intended.

The purpose of this volume is to illustrate the general historical setting of the narratives of the Old Testament and Christian times; to see how we must understand them as part of the history of the period; to see what consistent conclusion we can reach on taking into account all the circumstances; and to show the point of view of a general historian in regard to these narratives.

This position has the disadvantages of a middle course. Those whose criticism runs to proving every statement unhistorical, may resent the plain acceptance of documents and statements, wherever not modified or disproved by more certain sources. Even when statements in one part of a document contradict another part, I believe that it may generally be found that the accidental omission of an interval of time, or of a qualifying circumstance, has been the cause of the discrepancy. Misapprehensions and blunders of compilers are far commoner than sheer invention.

On the other hand, those who wish to accept entirely incompatible statements without comparison, may not relish the inevitable necessity of having to yield to historical consistency. They may be ready to revile the errors of a transcriber, while they yet cling to the infallibility of a compiler. Yet there is scarcely any historical statement in the Bible that has not been compiled—generally more than once—out of the editing of earlier documents. Statements which may have been minutely correct as originally written, are sure to suffer when they are subsequently condensed and fused into a more general narrative.

It will be evident that such a summary as this belongs mostly to the general reader; but those whose studies have already extended to the larger and more detailed works will also find fresh questions discussed here. This is intended as a general view of the subjects, rather than as a complete inquiry of detailed research.

CONTENTS

		PAGE
PREFACE	... ...	iii

CHAPTER
I. ABRAM, THE SHEPHERD PRINCE.

1.	The Decay before the Hyksos	...	...	11
2.	The Babylonian Kings of Egypt	...	...	12
	The Entry of the Hyksos ...	...	...	14
	The Migration from Ur	...	...	16
	The Nomad Civilisation	...	...	17
	The Hyksos Civilisation	...	...	18
	The Egyptians and Semites mixed	...	...	20
8.	The Mother of the Tribe	...	...	21
9.	The Famines	26

II. ISRAEL IN EGYPT.

10.	Contrast of Genesis and Exodus	...	...	28
11.	Conditions in Egypt ...	...	...	28
12.	The Brickmaking ...	...	...	31
13.	Positions of Store Cities	...	...	33
14.	Israel not all in Egypt	...	...	34
15.	The Plagues ...	...	...	35

III. THE EXODUS

16.	The Date...	37
17.	The Route	39
18.	The Numbers	40
19.	The Census Lists	42
20.	The History of Levi	46
21.	The Semitic Worship	47

CONTENTS

CHAPTER					PAGE
IV.	THE PERIOD OF JUDGES.				
	22. The Condition of Syria	...	...	...	50
	23. Limits of the Period	...	...	...	52
	24. The Triple History	...	...	...	54
	25. The Family Histories	...	...	...	55
	26. The Growth of Israel	...	...	...	57
	27. Egyptian Influence	...	...	...	60
V.	THE MONARCHY.				
	28. Hadad of Edom	...	...	...	64
	29. Pharaoh's Daughter	...	...	...	66
	30. Family Links of Egypt and Judah		...	...	68
	31. Shechem the Old Centre	...	...	...	70
	32. The Israelite View	...	...	...	70
	33. Shishak's Invasion	...	...	...	72
	34. Usarkon's Invasion	...	...	...	74
	35. Shabaka, the Viceroy	...	...	...	75
	36. Tirhakah, the Ethiopian	...	...	...	77
	37. Expeditions of Necho	...	...	...	78
VI.	THE CAPTIVITY.				
	38. The Three Captivities	...	...	...	81
	39. Permanence of the Population		...	...	82
	40. The Refugees in Egypt	...	...	...	84
	41. Position of Tehaphnehes	...	...	...	85
	42. Importance of Tehaphnehes		...	...	87
	43. The Babylonianizing Party	...	...	...	90
	44. The Prophecy of Jeremiah	...	...	...	91
	45. The Fate of Hophra	...	...	...	92
	46. The Jews of Syene	...	...	...	93
	47. The Earlier Type of Judaism		...	...	96
VII.	ISRAEL TRIUMPHANT IN EGYPT.				
	48. The Trouble in Judaea	...	...	...	97
	49. The Youth Oniah	...	...	...	98
	50. The Petition of Oniah	...	...	...	100
	51. Discovery of the Temple of Oniah		...	...	102
	52. The Courts and Approaches		...	...	103
	53. The Outer Wall	...	...	...	104

CONTENTS

CHAPTER		PAGE
VII.—ISRAEL TRIUMPHANT IN EGYPT—*continued*.		
54.	The Passover Ovens	105
55.	The Jewish Remains	107
56.	Authority of Josephus	108
57.	The New Jerusalem in Egypt	108
VIII. THE FORERUNNERS OF CHRISTIANITY.		
58.	The Growth of Thought	111
59.	The Hermetic Books	112
60.	Beliefs on the Godhead	113
61.	The Logos	114
62.	Types of Conversion	116
63.	Links with Christianity	117
64.	Pauline Use of the Book of Wisdom	118
IX. THE GROWTH OF THE GOSPELS.		
65.	The Light from the Logia	124
66.	The Nucleus of the Gospels	126
67.	How the Evangelists used the Documents	127
X. EGYPT AND CHRISTIANITY.		
68.	The Jewish Position	130
69.	The Source of the Agapé	131
70.	The Earliest Monasticism	133
71.	What was before Time	135
72.	The Madonna and the Bambino	137
DETAILED WORKS ON SUBJECTS		143
INDEX		145

LIST OF ILLUSTRATIONS

FIG.		PAGE
1.	CYLINDER OF KHENDY, BABYLONIAN KING OF EGYPT	12
2.	"THE PRINCE OF THE DESERT ABSHA," with an ibex, and his Syrian followers in coats of many colours; the forerunners of the Hyksos migration. They are armed with spears, bows, and throwsticks, carrying a waterskin slung on the shoulders, and playing on a lyre. Beni Hasan, XII Dynasty ... ... *Frontispiece*	
3.	BEDAWY TENT. A mere roof with some stalks round it on the windward side. In Syria, flaps of camel-hair cloth are hung to windward (p. 14) ... ... *Frontispiece*	
4.	SCARABS OF SEMQEN, ANTHER, AND KHYAN, HYKSOS KINGS OF EGYPT	15
5.	MAP OF PATRIARCHAL SITES ... ... *To face page*	16
6.	EARTHEN FORT OF THE HYKSOS AT TELL-EL-YEHUDIYEH	19
7.	MAP OF SITES BETWEEN EGYPT AND THE RED SEA ...	29
8.	VIEW OF THE RICH LAND OF GOSHEN. Corn on the ground and palm trees above ... ... *To face page*	30
9.	NAME OF ISRAEL FROM THE GREAT SLAB (Fig. 14). The hieroglyphs are "Ysiraal, people." *To face page*	30
10.	CURSIVE WRITING OF SEMITIC USE FROM SERABIT, 1400 B.C.	32
11.	MODERN EGYPTIANS MAKING BRICKS. Note the mat beyond the man for carrying the mud, the mound of mud, the water-pot for wetting the mould, the rows of bricks drying on the ground, and the dry bricks stacked on the right ... ... *To face page*	32
12.	CAPTIVES MAKING BRICKS ANCIENTLY. Note the mound of mud, the pan of water by the left moulder, the mould held by the right moulder, and the row of bricks on the ground. Thebes, XVIII Dynasty *To face page*	32
13.	RAMESES II SLAYING A SYRIAN: TEMPLE OF RAAMSES CITY	34
14.	GRANITE TRIUMPHAL SLAB OF MERENPTAH, naming his victories over the Libyans and in Palestine, "the people of Israel is spoiled it has no corn." At the top the god Amon in the middle, giving a falchion to the king, on each side; the goddess Mut behind the king on the left, the god Khonsu on the right *To face page*	34
15.	VIEW BY LAKE TIMSAH, showing the sand dunes around it. The crossing by the Israelites must have been near this place ... ... *To face page*	40

LIST OF ILLUSTRATIONS

FIG.   PAGE

16. THE WATERS OF ELIM IN THE WADY GHARANDEL, ON THE ROAD TO SINAI ... ... *To face page*   40
17. YOUNG PALM TREES IN A VALLEY NEAR ELIM *To face page*   40
18. MODEL OF THE TEMPLE AT SERABÎT. To the left, under the highest upright slab, is the rock cave, the original shrine. Before that are the courts of the temple, the approach to which was at first along the line of upright slabs in the foreground. Thothmes III built the high pylon seen in the middle; and later kings added in front of that the cells for dreamers, out to the right. All the chambers were roofed with stone *To face page*   46
19. THE MAIN COURT OF ABLUTIONS AT SERABÎT. The round basin of stone on the ground was surrounded by four pillars with heads of the goddess Hathor, which supported the roof ... ... *To face page*   48
20. BUSH OF THE WHITE BROOM (*retem*; translated as "juniper"), SINAI ... ... *To face page*   49
21. INCENSE ALTARS OF SANDSTONE FOUND IN THE ROCK SHRINE AT SERABÎT, SINAI ... ... *To face page*   49
22. METAL VASES MADE BY THE SYRIANS AND MEDITERRANEAN PEOPLE ABOUT 1500 B.C. ... *To face page*   52
23. SYRIAN FORTRESS ATTACKED BY EGYPTIANS CLIMBING UP A LADDER AND HEWING AT THE GATE. Note the projecting parapet for machicolation, the battlemented top, and the windows ... ... *To face page*   52
24. PLAN OF THE CITY WALLS OF LACHISH...   52
25. HEAD OF RAMESES II, from his statue at Turin *To face page*   54
26. HEAD OF MERENPTAH, from his statue at Cairo *To face page*   54
27. HEADS OF HITTITES, from Armenia ... ... *To face page*   58
28. HEADS OF AMORITES, from Syria. Akin to the North Africans ... ... *To face page*   58
29. PHILISTINES. Probably from Crete ... ... *To face page*   58
30. EGYPTIAN ARK OF A GOD, with figures of Truth spreading their wings over it. The large curved mass is the linen wrapper which covered the ark, and the upper frame is the section of the shrine in which it stood *To face page*   62
31. BORDER OF LOTUS FLOWERS AND SEED-VESSELS. Called by the Israelites "bells and pomegranates" *To face page*   62
32. HEAD OF KING SIAMEN, from Memphis ... *To face page*   64
33. HEAD OF KING SHESHENQ. "Shishak, King of Egypt" *To face page*   64
34. BEAD OF KING PASEBKHANU   65
35. CANOPIC JAR AND USHABTI OF QUEEN KARAMAT ...   69

FIG.		PAGE
36.	FIGURE OF THE GOD AMON HOLDING CAPTIVE THE CITIES OF JUDAH FOR SHISHAK ... *To face page*	72
37.	ONE OF THE HEADS OF THE CITIES, Jud-ha-malek (Jehud of the king, Josh. xix, 45), which is the third behind the knee of the god Amon ... ... *To face page*	72
38.	SCARAB OF SHISHAK, WITH THE UNITED NAME OF USARKON (ZERAH)	74
39.	FIGURE OF THE NILE GOD. Down the back from A to B is the important mention of "the king's son, Usarkon (Zerah), whose mother was Karamat, daughter of King Pasebkhanu," the sister-in-law of Solomon *To face page*	74
40.	HEAD OF SHABAKA. "So, King of Egypt" *To face page*	76
41.	HEAD OF TAHARQA. "Tirhakah, King of Ethiopia" *To face page*	76
42.	TRIUMPHAL SCARAB OF NECHO	79
43.	RESTORATION OF THE FORTRESS OF TEHAPHNEHES, OR DEFENEH. The entry is seen at the inner angle, and the pavement of brickwork before it ... *To face page*	88
44.	POTTERY OVEN FOR BAKING THE PASCHAL LAMB, at the base of the mound of the city of Oniah *To face page*	88
45.	GREEK VASE WITH HARES, FROM TEHAPHNEHES ...	89
46.	PLAN OF THE FORT OF TEHAPHNEHES, with the various periods of building marked by different shading *To face page*	92
47.	PLAN OF THE CITY OF ONIAH, AND THE ENCLOSURE OF THE TEMPLE ... ... *To face page*	104
48.	MODEL OF THE ABOVE, SHOWING THE RELATIVE HEIGHTS OF THE PARTS ... ... *To face page*	104
49.	MASSIVE STONE WALL OF THE EASTERN ENCLOSURE OF THE CITY OF ONIAH ... ... *To face page*	106
50.	"THE CHURCH OF THE CIRCUMCISION," showing that as late as 430 A.D. the Jewish and Gentile Churches were regarded as on a par ... ... *To face page*	130
51.	"THE CHURCH OF THE GENTILES." In the church of Santa Sabina, Rome ... ... *To face page*	132
52.	POTTERY FIGURE OF ISIS AND HORUS, AS A GIRL WITH AN INFANT. Painted with red and blue stripes *To face page*	136
53.	POTTERY FIGURE OF ISIS AND HORUS, with drapery over the head ... ... *To face page*	138
54.	POTTERY FIGURE OF ISIS AND HORUS, with the girdle tie of Isis, and the crown, lock of hair, and round vase of Horus; these prove that this is an entirely pagan figure, though probably of the fourth or fifth century A.D., and show how completely this type was established before being appropriated to the Madonna *To face page*	140

EGYPT AND ISRAEL

CHAPTER I

ABRAM, THE SHEPHERD PRINCE

1. *The Decay before the Hyksos.*

TO most readers the period of Abram suggests the beginnings of history; but in the long vista of Egypt it comes at the close of the fifth age of civilisation. After it there are but three more civilisations—the Empire, the Greek age, and the Arab age. This fifth age of Egypt is otherwise known as the Middle Kingdom, or the XIIth dynasty, and it flourished from about 2500 to 2200 B.C. Like all great civilisations, it afterward passed through various stages of decay. For some six centuries the country was slowly living on its past resources and glories, gradually falling apart and torn by internal quarrels, until the great Semitic invasion of the Hyksos about 1600 B.C.

The scarcity of original monuments, and the shortness of the reigns show clearly how Egypt was decaying in those six centuries. We can grasp the position better by comparing it with the later Roman period. During six centuries, from Augustus onward, Egypt was gradually exhausted, while Arab mercenaries were employed in the Roman army, until at last the Arabs burst in at 640 A.D. Similarly in the earlier times the Egyptians of the Middle Kingdom, during their long decay, had used Syro-Mesopotamian troops, who gradually gained authority.

2. *The Babylonian Kings of Egypt.*

Fortunately we have preserved to us a monument of one of the Syro-Mesopotamian intruders who rose to the throne of Egypt. His name appears as Khendy, on a cylinder of green jasper (Fig. 1). He

FIG. 1.—Cylinder of Khendy, Babylonian king of Egypt.

is shown wearing the double crown of Egypt, and the Egyptian waist cloth. He is entitled *ankh*, " the living," and he gives the sign of life to a Babylonian figure standing before him. Beyond the Mesopotamian is an Egyptian holding a papyrus plant. A row of four ibexes bounds the scene on one side, and a northern guilloche on the other. Thus the Syro-Mesopotamian origin is shown by the cylinder seal, its workmanship, the row of ibexes, guilloche, and Mesopotamian figure; while the Egyptian connection

ABRAM, THE SHEPHERD PRINCE 13

is clear in the crown and dress, the cartouche, the scattered hieroglyphs, and the Egyptian holding a papyrus.

Another Babylonian of the same age is king Khenzer, whose name is also found as that of a later Babylonian king, Khinziros or Yukin-ziru. A well-cut tablet, now in Paris, bears the name of Khenzer along with an Egyptian name which he adopted, Ra-ne-maat-ne-kha. This name is based on the name of one of the most celebrated kings of the XIIth dynasty, Ra-ne-maat, Amenemhat III. The tablet states that the repairs of temples and provision for the worship were being carried on, and gives the king the usual Egyptian titles. All this points to the Babylonian having come into Egypt while the country was still well ordered, soon after the XIIth dynasty, and shows that he acted as a regular Egyptian king. Some scarabs of this king are also known.

These reigns illustrate the entirely Egyptian position assumed by the earlier Babylonian immigrants, who came into Egypt probably as mercenaries, and stayed to rule. They were in much the same position as the barbarian invaders of Italy, such as Theodoric, Gothic chief and Roman emperor, who was soon after succeeded by a far ruder horde of other invaders. A painting of one of these "Princes of the desert," named Absha, coming into Egypt, is preserved in the well-known scene at Beni Hasan. Though a thousand years before Abram, he was one of the same race, and probably led much the same kind of life. It is therefore invaluable as an historical type of the great Semitic invasion (Fig. 2).

The fate of Egypt was like that of Rome; wheresoever defence is trusted to foreign troops they soon become the masters, and the power *de facto* becomes the power *de jure*. The Arab troops employed by the Romans to garrison Egypt, brought on in a few centuries the Arab conquest; and so in earlier times the Eastern troops in Egypt led the way to the earlier Semitic conquest, that of the Hyksos or Shepherd Princes. The names of the conquerors plainly show their Semitic origin, as is generally recognised.

3. *The Entry of the Hyksos.*

The fullest account that we have of the Hyksos is that which is preserved to us by Josephus in his Controversy with Apion. He extracted it from the history of Manetho, of which we have only bare lists preserved otherwise. He states that the Hyksos poured into Egypt for a century as successive waves of tribes, plundering and destroying. After that time of turmoil they became firmly established, and founded a definite monarchy. The six great Hyksos kings ruled for 260 or 284 years, from about 2540 to 2256 B.C. They are parallel to the great Khalifs of the Arab period; and as those ruled in Baghdad and Egypt, so also the Hyksos Khyan king of Egypt left his monument in Baghdad, pointing to a similar extent of rule (Fig. 4).

After the great kings there followed some centuries of fusion between Semites and Egyptians, as indicated by the references in Genesis, as well as by the obvious probabilities of the case. This later period lasted from about 2256 to 1738 B.C.

ABRAM, THE SHEPHERD PRINCE

The great movement of the Semitic peoples in the third millennium B.C. had been up the course of the Euphrates, and then down the pastoral plains at the back of Syria. It appears to have been a general racial drift like that of the Eastern races into the Roman Empire through the south of Russia, when a dozen different peoples poured in between 400 and 900 A.D. It is very possible that Syria had remained the home of the blond Amorites until this Semitic migration. At the beginning of this move-

FIG. 4.—Scarabs of Semqen, Anther, and Khyan, Hyksos kings of Egypt.

ment we have seen the intrusion of rulers from Babylonia; the later kings of Hyksos race were Semitic, and the obviously pastoral and nomadic nature of their civilisation agrees to this.

The Turanian race akin to the modern Mongols was known as Sumerian or Akkadian in Babylonia; it had civilised the Euphrates valley for some thousands of years, and produced a strong commercial and mathematical culture, which has stamped itself on all Western life since. The wandering Semite of the Arabian steppes had at last been drawn into this settled system of life; he had then conquered the Turanian, and under Sargon and Naram-sin (3800 B.C.) had headed the Babylonian monarchy.

4. *The Migration from Ur.*

The city of Ur, now known as Muqayyer, stood on the Arabian border of the Babylonian plain. It is about half-way from Babylon to the Persian Gulf at present; but at the time we are now describing the coast was much nearer to those cities. From its position it was naturally a Semitic centre, as there was only one other city, Eridu, on the Arabian side of the Euphrates. It was from Ur, at about 2300 or 2250 B.C. that the family of Terah wandered up to Haran in the north, near Edessa. This movement was like that which had been going on among the Semitic people in the previous centuries. It came just at the close of the age of the great Hyksos kings, when probably fresh tribes were pressing forward. It was then that the later Hyksos dynasty pushed into Egypt, and obtained a footing in Cyprus and the Mediterranean (Fig. 5).

Such a migration is not likely to have been made late in the life of Terah. The long ages from father to son which are recorded, are alike contrary to all human physiology and experience. They are probably to be understood as arising from the omission of unimportant generations. Just before this time, in the XIIth dynasty, there was a very precise chronology kept up; and this Egyptian custom may probably have been reflected by such an interest in other lands. If there were a regular outline of tribal history, which was summarised by later compilers, the omitted generations might soon be understood as implying a long interval between father and son; on that understanding the total ages would soon be

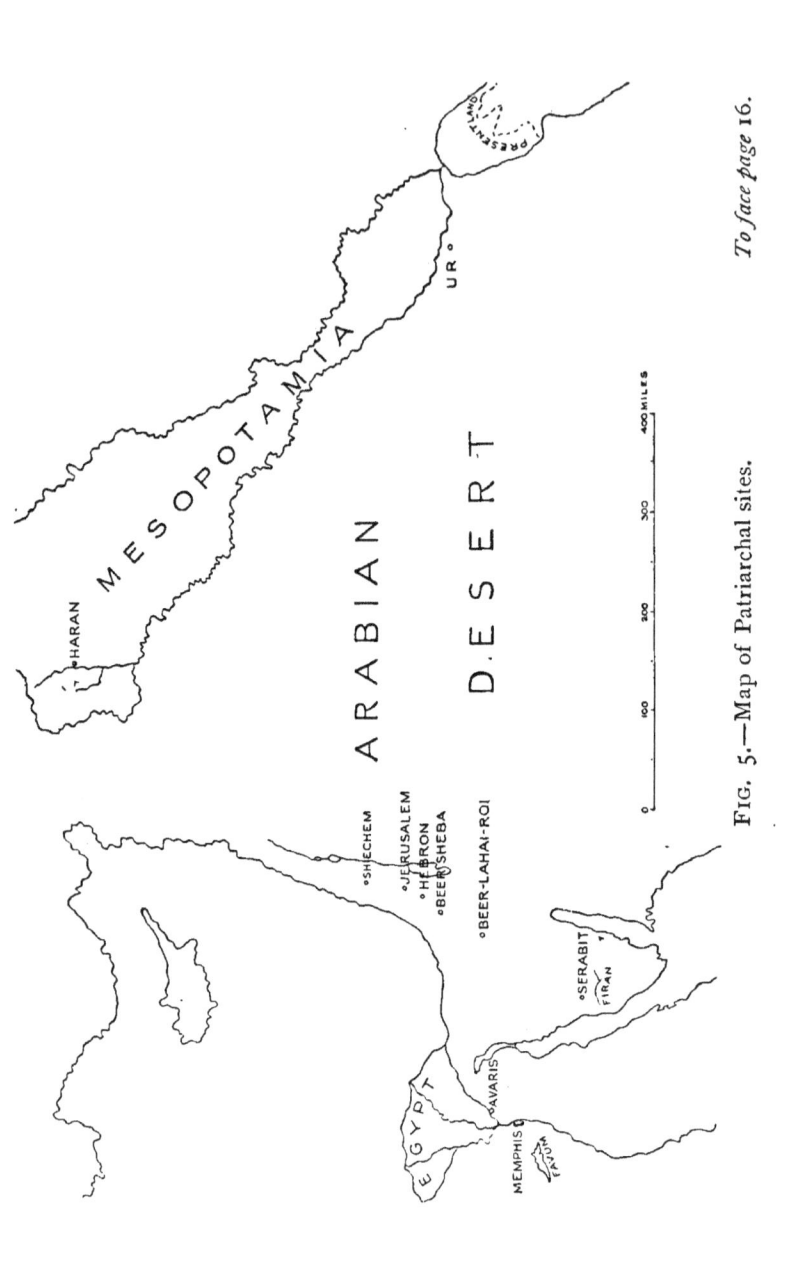

Fig. 5.—Map of Patriarchal sites.

To face page 16.

adjusted to fit the requirements. The shorter intervals of the generations from father to son, as the time was nearer, would be the natural result of more information being preserved about the more immediate ancestors. Hence we may reasonably accept the date of Terah as that of the migration of the family.

The period of Abram is most nearly fixed by the connection with Amraphael. The more usual view is that this King of Shinar is the same as Hammurabi, though he has been otherwise identified with Amarpal, the father of Hammurabi. The date of Hammurabi is probably about 2100 B.C.; and Abram was about 80 then. This would put the birth of Terah to about 2300 B.C., and his migration to about 2270 B.C.

Now, it was just about that time, 2256 B.C. according to the Egyptian history, that a fresh movement of the Semitic tribes took place, the great kings came to an end, and a new dynasty arose, numbered as the sixteenth. The migration of Terah was, then, part of a general movement of the kindred people at the time. Having now outlined the historical connections as nearly as we can trace them, we turn to the more living detail.

5. *The Nomad Civilisation.*

The beautiful episodes in Genesis picture to us the character of the civilisation. The people were nomadic, without any permanent dwellings, but always in tents; and often shifting from one pasture-land to another, over the whole of the hill country, for a hundred and twenty miles, from Shechem to

Beer-lahai-roi. No less than seven fluctuations, up or down along the ridge of hills, are named in the three generations of the patriarchs. Probably the whole stretch of country belonged to the clan, and was more or less occupied by them, as we see at the latter time that Jacob was living at Mamre, but had his flocks at Shechem, fifty miles north of him.

There is no trace of building named, nor of any wooden structures or furniture. Nor is there any ownership of a definite spot of ground mentioned, except for burial. The life must have been very closely what is seen at present in the black tents of the Bedawyn on the grassy hills of Judaea. Flocks and herds were the great wealth; but gold and silver were also recognised as wealth, and were treasured up. The sword and the bow were the characteristic weapons; this was contrary to the habit of the Egyptians, who, in fight, trusted to the battle-axe and the dagger, like our own forefathers.

6. *The Hyksos Civilisation.*

We are fortunately able to compare this civilisation with some points of the culture of the Hyksos. The discovery of their great fortress at Tell-el-Yehudiyeh, about twenty miles north of Cairo, has put before us somewhat of their life. This fortress consisted of an immense earth bank enclosing a square space of ground. The bank varies from 150 to 200 feet thick, and is 45 feet high; the space within it is a quarter of a mile square (Fig. 6). In all the defences there was no trace of the knowledge of stone or timber or brick walling. Strange to say, no entrance was constructed through the bank. The only way in was by a sloping causeway about 200 feet long, which led up to the top of the bank. This extraordinary and completely un-Egyptian construction shows that the makers were not accustomed to any settled habitation with regular building. It seems that they must have come in from a nomadic life on pastoral plains, destitute of wood for defences, and that their

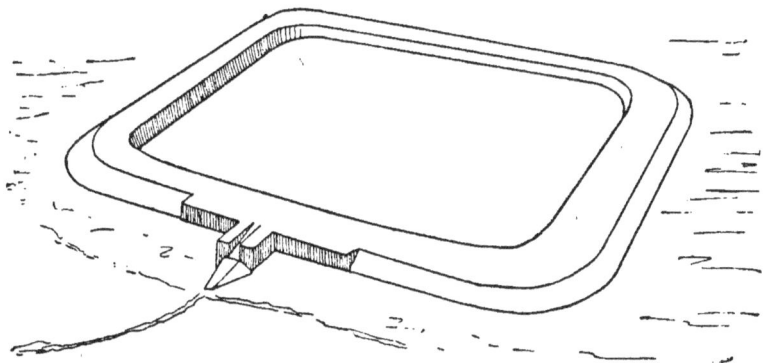

FIG. 6.—Earthen fort of the Hyksos at Tell-el-Yehudiyeh.

only idea of protection was an earthen bank and ditch.

The outer side of the bank was a long slope, running upwards for 50 to 70 feet, faced with mud and white plaster. The protection to the causeway entrance was not by any trap in it, but by throwing forward flanking walls in advance, so as to cover it more completely by archery. The whole principle of the defence was long-range archery, with a long *glacis* slope to ensure the full exposure of the enemy. That this system of defence was known in Syria is shown by the *glacis* on the south side of Tell Hesy, of the Jewish age.

This defence explains the somewhat puzzled account given by Manetho: "There came up from the east in a strange manner men of an ignoble race, who had the confidence to invade our country, and easily subdued it by their power without a battle." The archery of the Hyksos tribes entirely outranged the Egyptian means of attack and defence; strength, skill, and organisation were all useless if the enemy had long-range weapons. The Hyksos archers could exterminate any opposition as readily as Merenptah crushed the Libyan host with his superior archery, or Narses crushed the Frankish host of hand-fighters.

We see thus that in each point that we can trace there was a culture among the Shepherd Princes, the "princes of the deserts" as they are called, which was similar to the life that is shown in the accounts of the Patriarchs. The migrations of Abram were in the usual course of the movements of his kindred, multitudes of whom preceded and also followed him. He was received as a matter of course by the Hyksos ruler of Egypt, and he wandered to and fro in the Hyksos Syria and Egypt at his will.

7. *The Egyptians and Semites mixed.*

The Hyksos invasion seems to have had the effects which might be expected in the mixture of Egyptians and Semites. Hagar was an Egyptian, probably a slave bought by Abram, or presented to him, during his visit to Egypt. Ishmael, therefore, was half Egyptian. And his mother—true to her people—took an Egyptian wife for him. His main descendants, therefore, were three-quarters Egyptian, only quadroon Semites. They are later represented as occupying Gilead and Moab, and being herdsmen under the name of Hagarenes, Hagariim.

The ceremony of circumcision was an Egyptian custom as far back as two thousand years before Abram. It is shown on the early monuments, it is named by Herodotos, and it is still the custom of both Muslims and Christians. It is therefore noticeable that it was Ishmael, the son of the Egyptian Hagar, who was first circumcised by Abram, long before Isaac was born. The Egyptian influence seems evident in this custom, since adopted by Islam.

That the Egyptian connection was not merely that of the Semitic Hyksos, then termed Egyptians, is shown by the curious fact that the Egyptian language seems to have been used in the south of Palestine at Gerar. The general of the Semitic prince Abimelech was named Phichol. This is a well-known Egyptian name Pa-khal, meaning "the Syrian." The plain inference is that a *khali* or Syrian was looked on as of different race in Gerar, and that the Egyptian language was commonly known or spoken there.

8. *The Mother of the Tribe.*

There is perhaps nothing more awkward to most readers than to realise freely an entirely different standard of morality in another land or another age. The present standard is always asserting its claims over all others in their minds. A wholesome corrective is to know and respect a Muslim whose wives are invisible. Our standard would be as great a shock to his life as his standard would be if applied to ours. Now, the standard of the Patriarchal age differed greatly from ours at present, as polygamy was the recognised order of life, and the marriage with a half-sister was correct. There were also some other strange matters about the position of women, which have been overlooked in modern times, and which even the later Hebrews tried to explain as difficult incidents. The independent rights and action of the female head of an establishment, or mother of the tribe, can best be grasped by looking at other parallels.

It is in Sinai that we may perhaps see best the primitive western Semitic life at present; every other land has yielded to the gains of civilisation; in Sinai there is nothing to gain, and it is unaltered. Among the Bedawyn there the woman is the mistress of the tent and of the herds. She and her children alone occupy the tent; the men sleep in the open or under a rock or bush. She leads out the flocks all day to pasture; the man wanders far on business with his camel. She carries all the treasure upon her in silver anklets and armlets, and necklets and veil ornaments; the man has nothing. The business of the man is to fight and to travel. The woman is the mistress of the property and the family.

In earlier times the same importance is seen in the south of Palestine, where the Nabathaean coinage of Edom has not only the head of the king on one side, but also the head of the queen on the other

ABRAM, THE SHEPHERD PRINCE 23

side. At Palmyra the queen Zeynab—Zenobia—was much more important than Odeynat her husband, or Wahaballat her son.

In Egypt all property went in the female line, the woman was the mistress of the house; and in early tales she is represented as having entire control of herself and the place. Even in late times the husband made over all his property and future earnings to his wife in his marriage settlement. In Coptic days the woman as well as the man could repudiate their marriage and be divorced on paying a sum fixed in the marriage contract; and a Copt selling anything in the market had to add "with my wife's consent," to make the bargain valid.

This view of the position of women, both in Semitic and Egyptian life, enables us to see the connection of some very curious statements, which the later writers have glossed over and tried to explain away. Sarah is the feminine of *Sar*, a chief or prince, and is usually rendered "princess"; but in modern English the word "prince" has got the sense of descent without rule, so chieftain would be a better rendering. This chieftainess travelled from place to place, accompanied by her half-brother Abram. Twice she was taken into the palaces of rulers, both Pharaoh of Egypt and Abimelech of Gerar, with her full consent. Such places might have been avoided; Sarah need not have been seen, and (as the results show) Abram ran no danger in claiming her to be his wife. The account as it stands seems evidently to have been accommodated to a different standard of life by later writers. In the next generation exactly the same thing is done with Rebekah, who is declared independent of Isaac at Gerar.

Really these chieftainesses appear to have had but little tie to their Semitic husbands, and to have been quite ready to renounce them if a more civilised position was open to them. Sarah, we see, had an independent establishment at Mamre, where she died; and Abram lived at Beersheba, and "came to mourn for Sarah" and to bury her.

Isaac, her son, was not officially married till she was dead, though he was forty. It is not to be supposed that, in a time when polygamy was usual, a young Sheykh remained celibate till forty. The marriage to one of the kin, Rebekah, was the political marriage for the clan, to set up a fresh chieftainess after Sarah was dead. And, significantly, Isaac had removed his mother's tent, seventy miles from Mamre, down to his distant camp at Beer-lahai-roi, ready for the new head of the tribe. So soon as Rebekah came, "Isaac brought her into his mother Sarah's tent"; that is to say, the female next-of-kin was installed officially. After that was done he "took Rebekah, and she became his wife."

It seems not unlikely that the difficulty about Leah and Rachel was due to Leah being the legitimate successor to the tribal headship, and so being necessarily married to Jacob before he could have Rachel.

In the next generation we find only one daughter mentioned to eleven sons. And that daughter, Dinah, is the only daughter of the chieftainess Leah. She appears again, along with Serah, these being the only two women mentioned with sixty-eight men going down into Egypt. Obviously, it is impossible but that there were many other daughters and wives in the reputed seventy souls that went into Egypt; but none of them are noticed or counted except these two. What made them to be thus singled out, and reckoned different to all other women? Leah was the eldest; as such, she was the mother of the tribe, and Dinah, as her daughter, succeeded as tribal head. Her name Dinah, the feminine of Dan, a judge, may well refer to her position.

The fury of the Israelites when she married a Hivite was because the tribal head would be lost to them; and they insisted that the Hivites must be circumcised, in order to join the tribe of Israel, so as to bring back the hereditary female head to the tribe. The next step was to restore the line, failing another daughter of Leah, by the line of Leah's handmaid, apparently in a kind of legal position as substitute (Gen. xvi, 2). The handmaid Zilpah had a son Asher, whose daughter Serah seems to have been accepted as the ruling female, since she is the only woman named in her generation among those who went into Egypt. Her name is not readily explained as it stands, and it seems probable that it is a corruption of Sarah, the "chieftainess." The difference is *heth* instead of *he*, an easy error.

While in Egypt the female headship does not appear, unless it be in Miriam, who was a prophetess like Deborah, and who is the only woman named in the genealogies. The tribal mother was not extinguished, however, for in the age of Judges we read, "Deborah . . . judged Israel . . . and the children of Israel came up to her for judgment . . .

and she sent and called Barak . . . and said unto him . . . take with thee ten thousand men . . . and Deborah arose and went with Barak. . . . I, Deborah, arose . . . a mother in Israel." Here the mother of the tribe is again seen in full vigour, judging and directing the fighting. This title, "a mother in Israel," also re-appears later in similar use in David's time. A wise woman in the city of Abel, when besieged, demands to see Joab, the captain of the besiegers; she tells him that he seeks "to destroy a city and a mother in Israel"; she negotiates terms, directs the elders of the city, and makes peace. As Deborah was "a mother in Israel," so probably this other woman had the same position as female head of the people; certainly her action shows that she had much authority, and knew how to use it.

It seems, then, that beneath all the show of patriarchal rule there was a recognised position of a female head of the clan or tribe, which was carefully maintained in earlier times, and which lasted on to the age of the monarchy.

9. *The Famines.*

The recent studies of changes in Central Asia have led to the view that there are recurring periods of dryness, which naturally throw the nomad people upon the richer lands for sustenance, and cause frequent famines (Huntingdon, *Royal Geog. Soc.*, 1910). This generalisation greatly clears up the early history. The movement of the nomadic Hyksos, from the semi-arid plains of Northern Arabia into Egypt, was probably caused by increasing scarcity of food. After that came the famine in Canaan, as the dryness increased, which impelled the inhabitants toward Egypt. Then, lastly, the dryness affected Abyssinia, and there ensued the seven years' famine in Egypt itself. Similarly, some centuries after the Arab invasion of 640 A.D., there were famines in Egypt from 900 to 1300 A.D., the worst and longest during seven years in 1065 to 1072 A.D. That Joseph's period was in the Hyksos rule is shown by the Babylonian title given to him, Abrek, which is the Babylonian Abarakhu, who was one of the five great officers of state.

CHAPTER II

ISRAEL IN EGYPT

10. *Contrast of Genesis and Exodus.*

THE contrast is well marked when we look at the picture-narratives of Genesis, which are full of feeling and expression, as compared with the more dry and business-like accounts of Exodus. The one is the national epic of poetic traditions, the other is a documentary narrative expanded by its compilers and editors. In Exodus we come into touch with the use of surviving documents; they appear to have been often copied, interpolated with fresh matter, filled out with traditions which illustrate them, sometimes misunderstood and wrongly connected by the editors,—all that is evident. But by the very distractions of idea, and misfits of the narratives, it is evident that permanent material was being used.

11. *Conditions in Egypt.*

The conditions of the sojourn in Egypt should first be grasped. It is expressly stated that the Israelites were settled in the land of Goshen, in order to be out of the way of the Egyptians. But

Goshen is not a large tract of country; it is bounded on the north and south by deserts, which are too

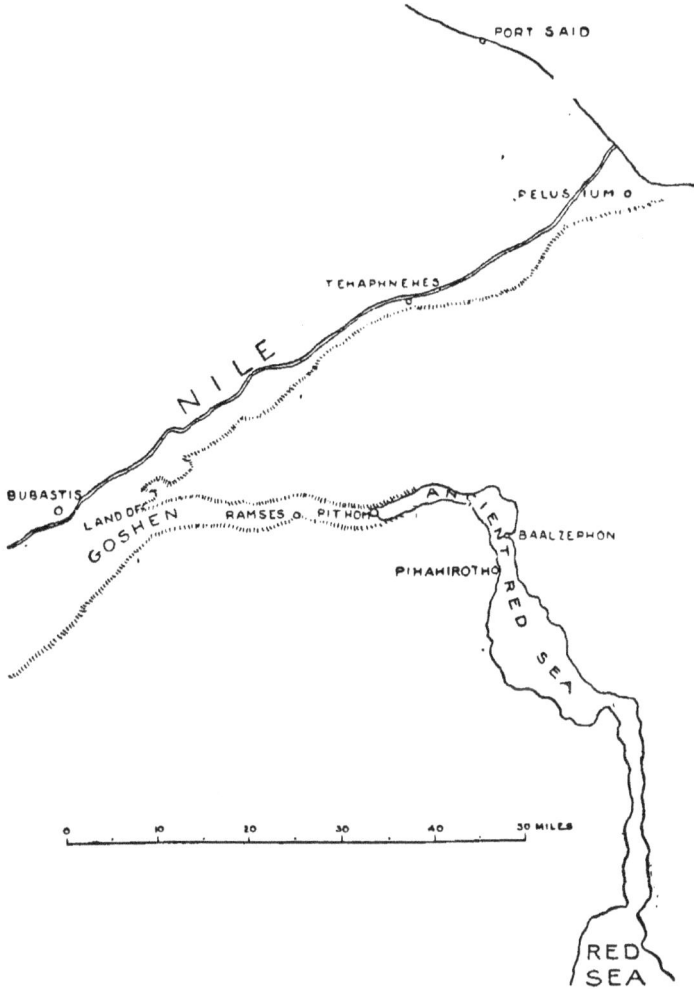

FIG. 7.—Map of sites between Egypt and the Red Sea.

high to have been cultivated; it dwindles to a mere channel on the east; and on the west it is barred by the great city of Bubastis, which was always an important centre of Egyptian life and worship. A triangle of about ten miles in the side, with perhaps some minor extensions, is all that can have been comprised in Goshen. If we make every possible allowance it cannot have covered 100 square miles (Fig. 7).

The population of this district is stated to have been 4000 Bedawyn a century ago; it is now improved by agriculture to support a farming population of 12,000 persons. As the Israelites were essentially pastoral, probably the Bedawy population shows most nearly what numbers Goshen formerly supported. The Israelites must have been much like the half-settled Bedawyn of the present day, living in tents scattered over the country, with their flocks and herds (Fig. 8).

If we take the Bedawyn as examples of such nomad life, we see that the Sheykhs may be very rich, with fine trappings, but yet using the wooden bowls and the leather waterskins which are most suited to a wandering life. The tent is usually open to the east; a low roof of black or brown camel hair is stretched over poles, with a flap down on three sides to keep off the wind. The sword and gun are hung upon the low tent-pole, as the sword and bow were anciently. A rush mat on the ground serves to sleep upon, and cooking is done on a smouldering fire of wood ashes in front of the tent (Fig. 3). Even after the occupation of Palestine, such a life was continued. We can see this on visiting the sites of the "towns" mentioned in the south of Judah; not a trace of pottery or of walls is to be found all

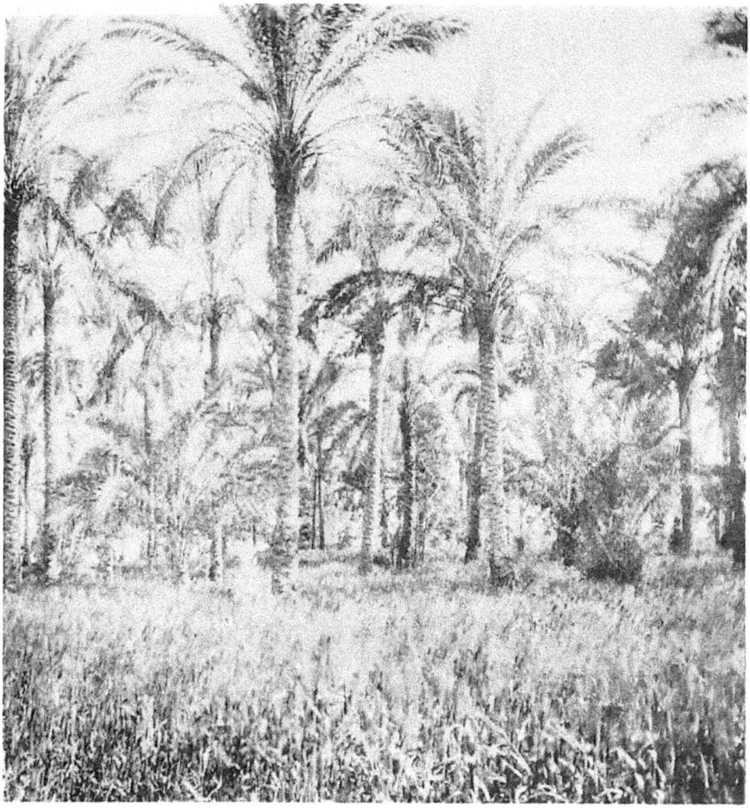

FIG. 8.—View of the rich land of Goshen. Corn on the ground and palm trees above.

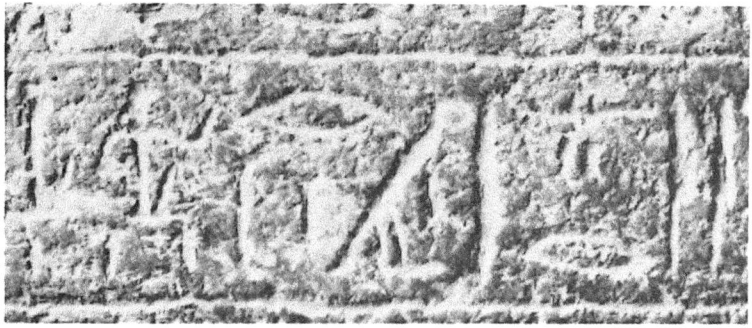

FIG. 9.—Name of Israel from the great slab (Fig. 14). The hieroglyphs are "Ysiraal, people."

To face page 30.

over the neighbourhood. Evidently skin and wood remained the domestic materials, and tents were the dwellings; and thus neither ruins of brick or stone, nor any potsherds, mark the site in after-ages.

12. *The Brickmaking.*

The levying of Israelites for forced labour by the Egyptians doubtless changed their conditions of life. They were probably housed close together in brick huts, as they were making bricks; and they were organised more exactly than formerly in the tribe. We read of the "officers (*shatar*) of the children of Israel which Pharaoh's taskmasters (*sarmas*) had set over them." And these officers said to Pharaoh, "Thy servants are beaten, but the fault is in thine own people." Hence clearly the officers were Israelites, and not Pharaoh's own people. The *shatar* means literally "scribe," but had early passed into the sense of a director, probably including the idea of a registrar. The *sar mas* or captains of tribute were the Egyptians, who directed the forced labour, and gave general orders. We see, then, that some of the Israelites were educated to control and direct the work of their own people. We also know, from the remains at Serabīt, that there was a native Semitic cursive writing before this time; there is, therefore, no reason to think that the Israelites were unable to keep record as overseers, in one form or another (Fig. 10).

The Israelites being settled in Goshen, the Egyptians when controlling them most naturally employed them in the defences of that part of the country.

So two fortresses were built blocking the eastern road into Egypt, in the Wady Tumilat, which runs between the Delta and the canal.

For these buildings, large quantities of mud bricks were needed; and such are always made as near as possible to the site required, as the cost of carrying them a mile is more than that of making them. The present routine for brickmaking is doubtless just the same as anciently. A hole is dug at the edge of a stream or pool, and the mud is trampled up in it. Sand or marl is usually mixed in to prevent cracking

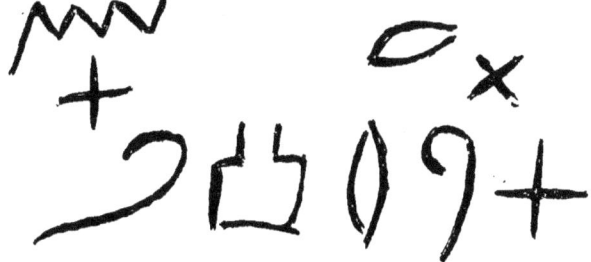

FIG. 10.—Cursive writing of Semitic use from Serabît, 1400 B.C.

in drying, and chopped straw from the threshing-floors, or grass stalks, may be mixed to bind the mud. Then a large lump of the mixture is taken out on a circular mat of palm-leaf, which serves to carry it upon. This is laid on a piece of ground swept smooth. The moulder next squats down, and takes a mass of mud large enough to fill his mould; he throws it in, presses it into the corners, smooths over the top so as to be level, and then lifts the mould carefully off the brick, leaving it on the ground. Then setting the mould by the side of the finished brick he moulds another. He thus leaves the ground

FIG. 11.—Modern Egyptians making bricks. Note the mat beyond the man for carrying the mud, the mound of mud, the water-pot for wetting the mould, the rows of bricks drying on the ground, and the dry bricks stacked on the right.

FIG. 12.—Captives making bricks anciently. Note the mound of mud, the pan of water by the left moulder, the mould held by the right moulder, and the row of bricks on the ground. Thebes, XVIII Dynasty.

To face page 32.

covered with moulded bricks about an inch apart. After three or four days they are dry enough to be turned up on end, and a few days more dry them sufficiently for building (Figs. 11, 12).

It is by no means essential to mix straw in the bricks, and most of the ancient and modern bricks do not contain straw. As the people demanded straw it is more likely that it was not for mixing in the brick, as that only adds to the labour of making a given number. But finely chopped straw, as from a threshing-floor, is very useful to dip the hand in to prevent mud sticking to it, also to dust over the ground, and to coat each lump of mud before dropping it in the mould, so as to prevent sticking at each stage, and to enable the work to go on quickly and easily. Thus the order, "There shall no straw be given you, yet shall ye deliver the tale of bricks," shows that the work would be slower and more difficult, owing to the lack of straw-dust coating; the demand would have no sense if it related to straw to be mixed with the brick.

13. *Positions of Store Cities.*

The positions of the fortresses which the Israelites were employed in building lie to the east of Goshen. The city of Rameses, now Tell Rotāb, is about twelve miles along the narrow marshy valley; and Pithom, now Tell-el-Maskhuta, is about ten miles further east. The city of Rameses is identified by remains of a town and temple built by Rameses II. A large scene from the temple front, representing Rameses slaying a Syrian, is now at Philadelphia

(Fig. 13). There is no other city of this date along the valley, except Pithom. An official here was "over the foreigners of Thuku" or Succoth, the general name of this land which was occupied with Bedawy "booths" or *succoth;* he probably was the superintendent of the Israelites. Pithom is identified

FIG. 13.—Rameses II slaying a Syrian : temple of Raamses city.

by the mention there of the temple of Tum or Atmu, Pa-Tum.

14. *Israel not all in Egypt.*

The questions as to whether the whole of the Israelites went into Egypt, and whether they all stayed there, are by no means clear. First there rises the question as to the supposed names Jacob-el

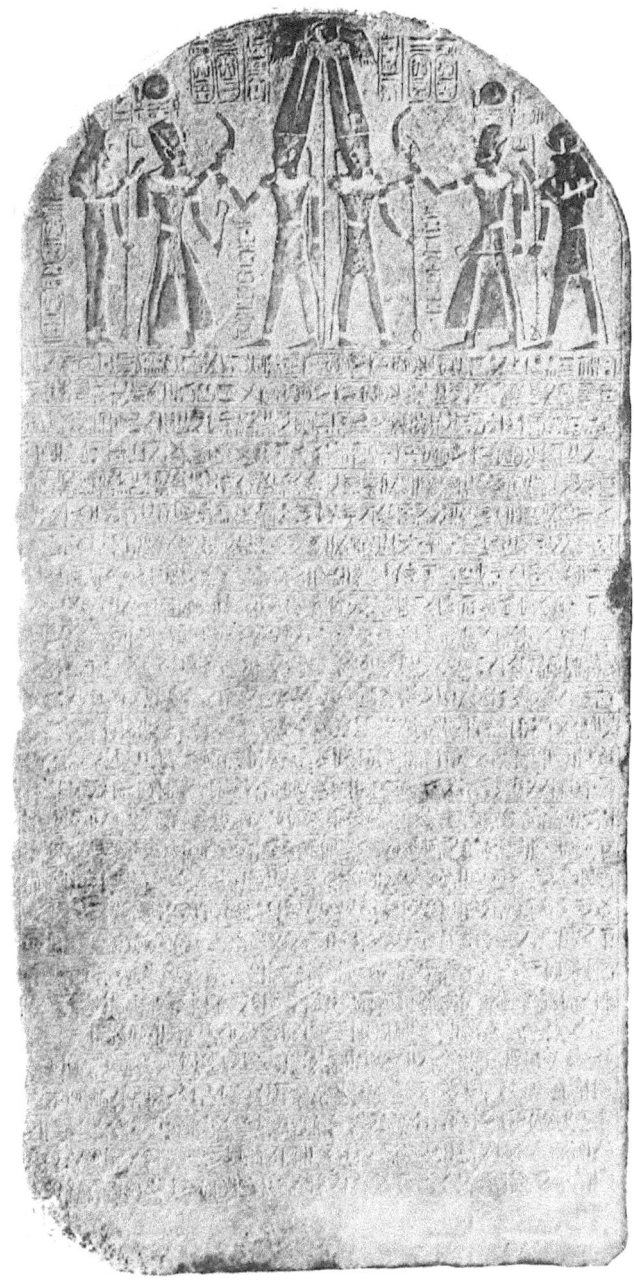

Fig. 14.—Granite triumphal slab of Merenptah, naming his victories over the Libyans and in Palestine, "the people of Israel is spoiled it has no corn." At the top the god Amon in the middle, giving a falchion to the king on each side; the goddess Mut behind the king on the left, the god Khonsu on the right.

and Joseph-el in the lists of people and places in the Syrian conquests of Tahutmes III, nearly three centuries before the Exodus. It has been thought that these represented tribes who were later incorporated in Israel, and gave rise to the names in Israelite history. But, if these names are correctly read—which is disputed—they might well be the names of divisions of Israelites who returned to their ancestral domains as soon as the famine was over. Similarly there is the great inscription of Merenptah, probably a few years before the Exodus, stating that in his Syrian war "the people of Israel is spoiled it has no corn" (or seed) (see Figs. 14 and 9). This shows that some Israelites were then in Palestine. We also read that during the residence in Egypt, raids were made up into Palestine (1 Chron. vii, 21). Another matter to note is that all the family sites were well known; whereas, if the whole people had been absent for 430 years from Palestine, the memory of the positions would have died out. It seems, then, probable that some Israelites continued in Palestine during most, or all, of the time that the others were in Egypt.

15. *The Plagues.*

The order of the plagues was the natural order of such troubles on a lesser scale in the Egyptian seasons, as was pointed out long ago. The river turned to blood, with the fish dying, was the unwholesome stagnant Nile just at the lowest before the inundation, when it is red and swarming with organisms. The Egyptians have to resort to wells and cisterns at this time in the earlier part of June. The frogs abound after the inundation has come in July. The plagues of insects, murrain, and boils, belong to the hot summer and damp unwholesome autumn. The hail and rain came in January. This is closely fixed by the effect on the crops. The barley must have been up early for the wheat to be yet "hidden" or hardly sprouting. This would show that it was planted early in November, in ear by the middle of January, and ripe early in March. The flax has like seasons, and the wheat is a month later. The locusts come in the spring, over the green crops about February. The sand storms bring a thick darkness that may be felt, in March, at the break of the hot winds. And the last plague, the death of the firstborn, was at the Exodus in April. An appeal based upon the troubles of these events, would be naturally denied on the ground that such plagues were to be expected at those seasons. The intervals are about a month apart; from the middle of January to mid April the time agrees to the months; but it seems impossible that the red Nile should be as late as the middle of July, so the scale of months cannot fit throughout exactly.

CHAPTER III

THE EXODUS

16. *The Date.*

THE question of the period of the Exodus has long been a subject of discussion. We must first see, therefore, what grounds there are for the earlier and later dates assigned to it.

The externally fixed points in the history are: (*a*) the entry of Abram into Canaan about 10 years before the Chedorlaomer war, fixed by the date of Khammurabi to about 2100 B.C., and (*b*) the building of the temple at 973 B.C. The extent of generations from Abram's entry to the descent into Egypt is $25 + 60 + 130$ years $= 215$ years (Gen. xii, 4; xxi, 5; xxv, 26; xlvii, 9). The sojourn in Egypt was 430 years (Ex. xii, 40); and from the Exodus to the temple was 480 years (1 Kings vi, 1). So far, the total is very close, $215 + 430 + 480 + 973 = 2098$ B.C. But when we come to apply this to fix the Exodus at 1453 B.C. the position is flatly contrary to the known history. For the names of the store city Raamses, and of the district "land of Rameses," show that the period must be after Rameses II (1300–1234 B.C.). Moreover, the Egyptians were incessantly raiding Palestine down to 1194 B.C., and yet there is absolutely no trace of Egyptian action in the whole period of the Judges, which shows that the entry into Canaan must be after that date. In the next chapter, on the Judges, we shall see that the actual statements of the Book of Judges, and the priestly genealogies agree to this later date. How this contradiction arose we can reasonably trace somewhat as follows. Having the above total from Abram to the temple known in general history, the later compilers took the periods in the Book of Judges as all cumulative, and hence went back 480 years to the Exodus. There was probably a strong tradition of the 430 years in Egypt, and the remainder was put into the darkest part of the history, in the long lives attributed to the Patriarchs. From the whole of the data we should space the history approximately thus:—

Abram's entry into Canaan	2110 B.C.
Israelite entry into Egypt	1650
Beginning of oppression	1580
Exodus	1220
Temple	973

The period of oppression is stated at four centuries (Gen. xv, 13; Acts vii, 6). Such a rise of an adverse rule would not occur under the kindred Hyksos, and they were not expelled from the Delta till the fifth year of Aahmes I, 1582 B.C. Hence the oppression is not likely to have been till 1580 B.C., and this leaves 360 years till the Exodus, which is roundly stated as four centuries. This period of the oppression after the close of the Hyksos rule entirely excludes an earlier date for the Exodus.

THE EXODUS

17. *The Route.*

Regarding the route of the Exodus there have been three views: (*a*) the northern line by Qantara, proposed by Brugsch, and now abandoned; (*b*) the line *via* Suez, and across the Sinai peninsula to Aqabah,—this was supposed to be needful to reach the Midianites, but there is no proof that Midianites may not have been in Sinai at the time; (*c*) the traditional route by the gulf of Suez, which agrees with all the indications, and which we shall describe here.

The Israelites are represented as having concentrated at Rameses, and immediately after the Passover marched to Succoth. This was a general name for the district of Bedawy booths in the Wady Tumilat the Thuku of the Egyptians. Thence they went to Etham in the edge of the wilderness, which would be about the modern Nefisheh. Thence they are said to turn and encamp before Pi-hahiroth, that is in Egyptian Pa-qaheret, where there was a shrine of Osiris, the Serapeum of later times; they turned from the eastern direction southward to this. There was a Migdol tower behind them, and Baal-zephon opposite to them. Here they were "entangled in the land, the wilderness had shut them in," as they had not rounded the north of the lakes. Formerly the gulf of Suez extended up through the lakes past Ismailiyeh to Ero, otherwise Pithom. They were thus "encamping by the sea, beside Pi-hahiroth." This is the highest ground between Ismailiyeh and Suez at present, and must have been the shallowest part of the former gulf. Here "a strong east wind all that night made the sea dry, and the waters were divided," so that it was possible to cross the gulf and reach Baal-zephon on the eastern shore (Fig. 15). After crossing they "went three days' journey in the wilderness of Etham, and pitched in Marah" (Num. xxxiii, 8). This is the road of three days' journey, which is defined as such by the absence of any water, and which was the avowed objective named to the Egyptians (Ex. v, 3). It is the marked feature of the Sinai road, and differs entirely from the seven days journey without water to Aqabah. At Marah the bitter water identifies it with the present bitter spring of the Wady Hawara. Two hours further on is the Wady Gharandel, where there is an excellent running stream and palm trees, agreeing to the well-watered Elim (Fig. 16). From thence they encamped by the Red Sea, again agreeing to this route. Thence they went into the Wilderness of Sin between Elim and Sinai; they passed Dophkah and Alush, not now identified, and came to Rephidim, where the main battle took place with the Amalekites for possession of the only fertile strip in the peninsula, the present Wady Feiran. It is obvious that this route was well known to the writers of the itineraries in Exodus and Numbers, and there is no discrepancy or question left in the matter.

18. *The Numbers.*

An essential question in any consideration of the Exodus, is that of the numbers of the people. A very serious difficulty has been felt by every one who has considered the statements of numbers; and the

FIG. 15.—View by Lake Timsah, showing the sand dunes around it. The crossing by the Israelites must have been near this place.

FIG. 16.—The waters of Elim in the Wady Gharandel, on the road to Sinai.

FIG. 17.—Young palm trees in a valley near Elim.

To face page 40.

cannot have exceeded this amount. How could the Israelites have had any appreciable resistance from a poor desert folk, if they outnumbered them as a hundred to one? Again, we are compelled to suppose that the Israelites were not more than a few thousand altogether. Thus we see that more cannot be got out of Goshen or into Sinai.

19. *The Census Lists.*

The whole basis of the total numbers stated, is the census of the tribes given in Numbers at the time of the Exodus. And this is checked by the second census given in Numbers xxvi, later in the wanderings. These lists are the material which needs to be understood.

	Num. i.	Num. xxvi.
Reuben	46,500	43,730
Simeon	59,300	22,200
Gad	45,650	40,500
Judah	74,600	76,500
Issachar	54,400	64,300
Zebulon	57,400	60,500
Ephraim	40,500	M. 52,700
Manasseh	32,200	E. 32,500
Benjamin	35,400	45,600
Dan	62,700	64,400
Asher	41,500	53,400
Naphtali	53,400	45,400

The only difference in the order of the lists is that Manasseh and Ephraim are interchanged, marked M. and E.; but as the numbers are most alike as they stand, it is probable that only the names have been interchanged. Now on looking at these lists a remarkable feature is that the hundreds of the numbers are mostly 4 or 5; 14 out of 24 numbers fall on these two digits, and there is not a single hundred

THE EXODUS

on 0, 1, 8, or 9. If we count up the examples of each hundred they come out thus—

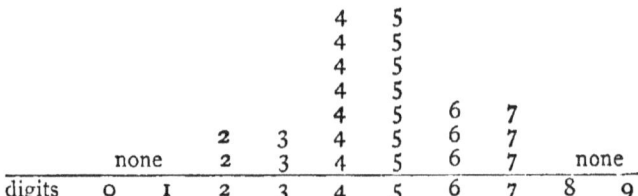

There is here clearly some selective cause why the hundreds group together on 4 and 5, and around those digits, while avoiding both the extremes. This can only mean that the hundreds are independent numbers in some way, and not merely the odd amounts after the thousands. Can either the hundreds or the thousands mean anything else?

The word translated here as thousands is *aláf*; and this has two meanings—"a thousand," and "a group" or "family." Hence the statement in words of 32 *aláf* 2 hundred people might mean 32 thousand 2 hundred, or 32 families 2 hundred people. In the latter sense the column of thousands would be the numbers of tents in a tribe, and the column of hundreds the numbers of people.

Now, this can be tested in two ways: (1) by the number of persons per tent, which should not be absurd, as there is no other enforced relation between the number of thousands, or tents, and hundreds; (2) by the number of hundreds being similar in both census lists, at least as much so as the thousands or tents.

The number of persons per tent might work out at 22 tents for 730 people, 33 per tent, or else at 76 tents for 300 people, or less than 3 per tent, if there were no real connection in the numbers. But, on the contrary, we find a general relation between the numbers in both census lists, which need not be at all alike if there were no real connection. The figures are as follows :—

	Census 1.			Census 2.		
	Tents.	Nos.	Per Tent.	Tents.	Nos.	Per Tent.
Reuben	46	500	11	43	730	17
Simeon	59	300	5	22	200	9
Gad	45	650	14	40	500	12
Judah	74	600	8	76	500	7
Issachar	54	400	7	64	300	5
Zebulon	57	400	7	60	500	8
Ephraim	40	500	12	52	700	13
Manasseh	32	200	6	32	500	16
Benjamin	35	400	11	45	600	13
Dan	62	700	11	64	400	6
Asher	41	500	12	53	400	8
Naphtali	53	400	8	45	400	9
	598	5550	9·3	596	5730	9·6

This shows that the average tent group was nine persons, which might well be two parents, two grandparents, three children, and two herdsmen, or hangers-on, of the "mixed multitude" who went with them. The poorest tribe had an average of five, which implied two parents and three children, the minimum that could keep up the tribe. The richer tribes had more children and many retainers. But there is nothing that is at all unlikely in the numbers of each tent group.

THE EXODUS 45

The other test is that the size of the tent groups of persons should not pass from one extreme to the other in the period between the two census lists. The greater part of the tribes remained at much the same level of group. Reuben, Simeon, and Manasseh show an increase in the tent group, while Dan and Asher show a decrease. The reason of the large decrease in tents, as well as numbers, in Simeon is because that tribe was concerned in the plague of Baal Peor, when twenty-four tent groups, or *aláf*, were swept off. The changes in the hundreds between the two lists is no more than might be expected in the course of over a generation, and there are no changes so considerable as we might expect were these merely chance numbers without any real connection.

Lastly, the result for the total number, 5550 people, is quite in accord with the general number that might come out of Goshen, or that would be only just a match for the scanty population of Sinai. This proposed understanding of how the impossible numbers have arisen is, therefore, perfectly consistent in its internal evidence and in its external connection, and the facts about the hundreds cannot be explained otherwise.

With this explanation of the meaning of *alaf*, as tent groups, we see other high numbers of the desert period appear reasonable. The plague (Numb. xvi, 49), which swept off 14 groups, 700 people in all, would show that 14 whole families perished, comprising about 130 people, and 570 other people singly out of other families. The other plague (Numb. xxv, 9), when 24 *aláf* perished, is also a likely result, as the tents of Simeon, the tribe concerned, fell from 59 to 22 at the later census.

There are two minor indications of the total numbers. Moses judged all disputes, which might be possible among 600 tents, but not among 600,000 men; and two midwives were employed (probably one at Pithom and one at Raamses), at the rate of one birth a week, according to the lesser number that we have found, while there would have been 140 births a day on the greater number stated.

20. *The History of Levi.*

In another respect we see that some entirely different solution of numbers must be found. The Levites are stated to be 22,000, made up of 7500 Gershonites, 8600 Kohathites, and 6200 Merarites. Here the *aláf* cannot be tent groups. But no more can the total of the firstborn (22,273) agree to either the 5550 population that we have found, or the gross reckoning of 600,000 men. The whole subject of Levites and firstborn cannot fit anything in the Exodus period. But it might well fit to the population when there were about 300,000 in Palestine. The dedication of firstborn would be likely to arise in Palestine, as the Canaanites sacrificed them; and the separation of a sacred caste would also be a gradual growth. We must look, then, to the time of the Judges as the source of these changes, and of the census document of Levi, which was incorporated afterwards in the Book of Numbers.

If there was no tribe of Levi at the time of the Exodus, it accounts for Levi being merely coupled

FIG. 18.—Model of the temple at Serabit. To the left, under the highest upright slab, is the rock cave, the original shrine. Before that are the courts of the temple, the approach to which was at first along the line of upright slabs in the foreground. Thothmes III built the high pylon seen in the middle; and later kings added in front of that the cells for dreamers, out to the right. All the chambers were roofed with stone. *To face page 46.*

THE EXODUS 47

with Simeon in the blessing of Jacob, and being given nothing but bitter reproaches and curses, such as could scarcely have been allotted to the holiest of the tribes. Simeon really was addressed alone, like the other tribes; and then Levi was joined in the blessing when instituted later, owing to their recognised association (Gen. xxix, 33, 34). The blessing of Jacob is therefore earlier than the institution of Levi; and it can be put before the first census, as in that Manasseh and Ephraim are separate, whereas the blessing treats them in one, as Joseph. It is thus seen to belong to the Egyptian period.

21. *The Semitic Worship.*

The nature of the changes introduced into the religion of the Israelites by the Mosaic system has been somewhat explained by the remains in a temple for Semitic worship, built in Sinai at Serabīt al Khādem. Though constructed by the Egyptians, who went there to mine the turquoise, the character of the ritual was in each respect not Egyptian, but adapted to the Semitic nature of the goddess. They worshipped according to "the manner of the god of the land," as Shalmaneser said. As these remains date before the Exodus, and some of them were ancient even then, we can see what were the elements of Semitic worship before the Mosaic system (Fig. 18).

The shrine was a cave, in front of which a court was added. This was on the top of a rise on a high plateau, overlooking miles of country below. Before the shrine lay an enormous amount of ashes, left from the burnt-offerings made on the hill, showing that the custom of sacrifice upon the high place was a main feature. This was continued in Israel by the orthodox, as the people all sacrificed in high places until the temple was built; and even then Solomon sacrificed and burnt incense in high places, and particularly at Gibeon, as that was the great high place (1 Kings iii, 3). The unorthodox kept up the custom till the Captivity.

Incense was offered upon small upright altars, placed within the shrine. This was the Jewish system, in which the altar of incense was the smallest, and stood within the most holy place (Fig. 21).

There were three sandstone tanks for ablutions of worshippers. One long rectangular tank outside the temple door; a second tank, circular, within a special court, surrounded by four pillars; a third tank, rectangular, in a further court with four pillars. These successive tanks were probably for the washing of different parts of the person, in course of entering. The performance of ablutions within the holy court in front of the most holy place is exactly what took place at the laver and the brazen sea, in a court where it was even death for a Gentile to enter. So in modern Islam, the great tank, or *hanafiyeh*, is in the midst of the main court (Fig. 19).

The Muslim ablutions are a portion of the religious service, regulated in the minutest particulars, accompanied by prayers, and forming a large part of the ordinary devotions. The presence of the tanks in the courts of the Sinai temple is therefore strictly the precedent for both Jewish and Muslim ritual.

Conical stones were found in the shrine; these are a well-known feature of Syrian worship, still

Fig. 19.—The main court of ablutions at Serabīt. The round basin of stone on the ground was surrounded by four pillars with heads of the goddess Hathor, which supported the roof.

To face page 48.

FIG. 20.—Bush of the white broom (*retem*; translated as "juniper"), Sinai.

FIG. 21.—Incense altars of sandstone found in the rock shrine at Serabīt, Sinai.

THE EXODUS

maintained in Islam with its black stone of the Kaabah, though omitted in Mosaism.

Sleeping places before the temple were built for those who dreamed there, to get oracular replies regarding the mining of turquoise. This custom, though only slightly referred to in the Old Testament, in connection with Bethel stones and with seers, was yet kept up by the Jews, even after the Captivity, as Strabo says that there was a class of official dreamers in the temple at Jerusalem in his time.

Thus the sacrifices, incense offering, ablutions, and Bethel dreaming were all older than Mosaism, and show how the old Semitic worship was not abolished but reformed in the Jewish system. The heathenism continually attacked by the orthodox teachers and prophets, was only the popular retention of more ritual than was favoured in the monotheistic religion at Jerusalem.

CHAPTER IV

THE PERIOD OF JUDGES

22. *The Condition of Syria.*

BEFORE we can understand the conquest of Palestine by the Israelites, we must note the condition of the land at that time. Syria had long been subject to Egypt. King Aahmes in 1582 B.C. had entered the south at Sharuhen, after ejecting the Hyksos; and Tahutmes I had conquered the whole country up to the Euphrates by about 1530. Fifty years later began the systematic plunder of Syria by raids and tribute, fourteen expeditions being recorded by Tahutmes III, between 1481 and 1462 B.C.; these cleared the country of all the valuables, and even of the crops. We see from the annals how high a civilisation there was among the Syrians; the metal vases, which are the principal objects of record, are finer than those which the Egyptians were making, and the Syrian artists were brought to work in Egypt (Fig. 22). Each succeeding king kept his hold on the country as tributary, until it revolted under the weak reign of Amenhotep IV, about 1370 B.C. Sety I reconquered the whole up to the Euphrates in 1326, and his son, Rameses II, continued to hold it till at

THE PERIOD OF JUDGES 51

least 1292 or later. He afterward lost his hold, but the south was regained up to Tyre in 1230 by Merenptah. Though lost again in the weak reigns of his successors, Palestine was reconquered in 1195 by Rameses III, when he crushed the Amorites. After this there was a long peace on the Egyptian border till Shishak in 933 plundered Judaea; and this interval between 1195 and 933 must comprise the early history of the Israelites in Canaan.

The frequent plundering by warfare and draining by tribute must have exhausted the country very seriously; and under Rameses III, the great league headed by the Amorites called forth all the possible reserves of wealth. All this was finally wrecked by the defeat, which left Rameses free to massacre and plunder everything of his enemies' which he could find. It was no wonder if, after such exhaustion, the country could not repel the band of hardy desert warriors, which burst in from Moab under Joshua. The manner in which the land had been bled is shown by the absence of all gold and silver in the spoils taken by the Israelites, except a small quantity on the eastern border at Jericho.

Of the cities of Syria, "walled and very great," there are many representations. In the plains, the walls were of brickwork, with many buttresses for strength and defence, as we see both on the sculptures and in the actual plans. The upper parts were carried forward, as a projecting story upon beams, much like houses in Northern Egypt to-day. This gave a complete protection to the defenders, from which they could drop missiles upon the enemy who might be injuring the wall. Against such defences the wandering tribes had no means of attack. Jericho was apparently betrayed by the house on the wall. Ai and Bethel were taken by a false flight drawing the defenders out. Gibeon made a treaty. The Amorite league was slaughtered in the field, leaving the five great cities defenceless. The men of Hazor

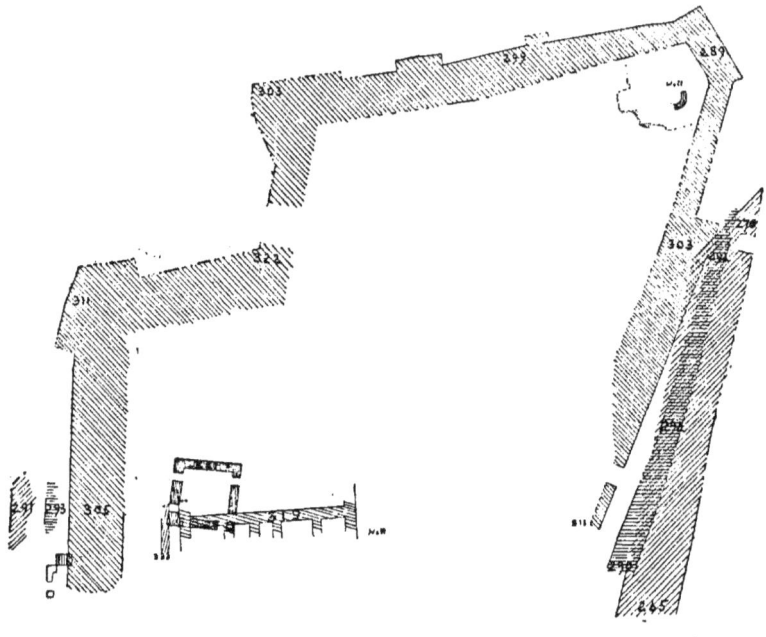

Fig. 24.—Plan of the city walls of Lachish.

and other cities were also defeated in the field, and their cities thus fell. In not a single case was a siege attempted (Figs. 23, 24).

23. *Limits of the Period.*

We have seen that the Egyptian evidence makes it almost impossible to suppose that the Israelites were in

Fig. 22.—Metal vases made by the Syrians and Mediterranean people about 1500 B C.

THE PERIOD OF JUDGES 53

Palestine before 1194 B.C., which was the date of the last Egyptian campaign there for two and a half centuries. Taking the traditional forty years in the wilderness, the Exodus would not be before 1234 B.C. Yet as Merenptah came to the throne that year, and had already had a campaign in Palestine by 1230, it is not likely that he would then have let the Israelites escape. It is to the latter years of his reign, which lasted till 1214, or during the confusion of his successors down to 1203, that the people of Goshen are more likely to have left. We may say, then, that 1220 B.C., or possibly rather later, is the date of the Exodus; and that 1180 B.C. would have been the end of the wanderings, when Israel spread in the fertile plains of Moab (Fig. 26).

The termination of the age of Judges by the rise of Saul, is the other limit which we must observe. From the Jewish and Assyrian chronology the death of Solomon is fairly fixed at 937 B.C. Accepting the traditional round number of 40 years each for the reigns of David and Solomon—which certainly were long—that would put Saul's death to 1017 B.C. The reign of Saul is over-estimated, owing to the use of 40 years in Acts xiii, 21. But it cannot have been long. In Saul's second year he was warned that his successor was already chosen (1 Sam. xiii, 14). David was by that time a solitary shepherd, able to slay wild beasts, and can hardly have been less than twenty years old. And David was only thirty years old at Saul's death. Thus there is only about three years before David's selection, and ten years after that, or thirteen years in all for Saul's reign. This would place him 1030-1017 B.C. Hence from the close of the wanderings to the rise of Saul there is only 1180-1030, or 150 years.

24. *The Triple History.*

Now, when we examine the history of the Book of Judges we shall find that there are three different districts named: (1) the North and Galilee; (2) the East, Gilead and Moab; (3) the West and Ephraim. Each judge is said to have ruled over one of these districts, but never over more than one district. They may have fought against another district, but they did not rule over it as judge. The different districts, with the approximate dates counting back from Saul at 1030 B.C., may be tabulated as on p. 55, with references to the Book of Judges.

It will thus be seen that when the judgeships and the periods of the history are separately classed to their respective districts, the total length of history is closely the same in each district. The interval from 1180 to 1150 B.C. was occupied in the plains of Moab and in the actual conquest. Joshua is represented as being the leader in war at the time of the Exodus, presumably about 40 years old; at the end of the wanderings he would be 80, and he is said to be 110 at his death, which leaves about 30 years for the sojourn in Moab and the conquest, in accordance with the interval which we have noticed above. There is no discrepancy in these dates, though that may not prove their original exactness.

The construction of the Book of Judges therefore begins with a brief episode of northern history (1148 to 1140); it then follows the order of the eastern,

FIG. 25.—Head of Rameses II, from his statue at Turin.

FIG. 26.—Head of Merenptah, from his statue at Cairo.

To face page 54.

THE PERIOD OF JUDGES

northern, and western divisions to more than half-way through, after which it repeats again the same order to the end.

The Different Districts.

NORTH.	EAST.	WEST.
B.C.	B.C.	B.C.
	1152 Eglon of Moab 18 years (iii, 14).	
1148 Chushan of Naharain rules 8 years (iii, 8).		1151 Midian holds up to Jezreel 7 years (vi, 1).
1140 Othniel delivers; rest 40 years (iii, 11).	1134 Ehud delivers; rest 80 years (including Jair below (iii, 30).	1144 Gideon delivers; rest 40 years (viii, 28).
1100 Jabin rules by Sisera, 20 years (iv, 3).		1104 Abimelech king in Shechem 3 years (ix, 22).
1080 Sisera slain; rest 40 years (v, 31).		1101 Tola judges 23 years (x, 2).
	1076 Jair judges; 22 years rest (x, 3).	1078 Abdon judges 8 years in N. (xii, 14). Ibzan judges 7 years in S. (xii, 9).
		1070 Philistines oppress 40 years (xiii, 1), including Samson 20 years (xv, 20).
	1054 Philistines and Ammon oppress, 18 years (x, 8).	
1040 Elon judges 10 years (xii, 11).	1036 Jephthah judges 6 years (xii, 7).	1050 and Samuel, judges 20 years (1 Sam. iv, 4; vii, 2; 2 Sam. vi, 2).
1030 Saul.	1030 Saul.	1030 Saul.

25. *The Family Histories.*

The evidence of these judgeships in different districts accords with the lengths of the genealogies. There are four priestly genealogies in 1 Chron. vi, one of which is also in 1 Sam. i, 1. References here given are to verses in 1 Chron. vi.

4–8	22–28, 33–35	39–43	44–47
Aaron	Korah	Shimei	Mahli
Eleazar	Assir	Zimmah	Shamer
Phinehas	Elkanah	Ethan	Bani
Abishua	Zophai	Adaiah	Amzi
Bukki	Nahath	Zerah	Hilkiah
Uzzi	Eliab	Ethni	Amaziah
Zerahiah	Jeroham	Malchiah	Hashabiah
Meraioth	Elkanah	Baaseiah	Malluch
Amariah	Samuel	Michael	Abdi
Ahitub	Joel	Shimea	Kishi
Zadok	Heman	Berachiah	Ethan
		Asaph	

Of these genealogies the heads—Aaron, Korah, Shimei (Ex. vi, 17), and Mahli (Ex. vi, 19)—were the heads of families at the Exodus, all fourth from the reputed ancestor Levi. (Note that Korah's children were not killed, Num. xxvi, 11.) At the other end, Zadok, Heman, Asaph, and Ethan were all the heads of families in the earlier years of David (1 Chron. xv, 17), when he established the ark services at about his fourteenth year, 1003 B.C. There are thus ten generations (or eleven in the line of Asaph), between the active men of the Exodus and of David's time. The period of eldest-son generation is best fixed by the certain series of Jewish kings, Rehoboam to Jehoiakin, sixteen generations in 937–598 years, or 339 years, averaging twenty-one years. The ten generations will, then, have occupied 210 years; and this taken back from David's date of 1003 B.C. gives 1213 B.C. for the Exodus, or by Asaph's line 1234 B.C. Thus, within the uncertainties of the length of the active period of a life, the four priestly genealogies, which are most likely to have been accurately preserved, all agree

THE PERIOD OF JUDGES 57

with the date that we have already reached for the Exodus. This evidence then fully confirms the shorter period for the Judges.

26. *The Growth of Israel.*

We now come to the difficult matter of the recorded numbers of the Israelites down to the monarchy. Too often it has been said that all high numbers are exaggerated and quite untrustworthy. But it is more satisfactory to see how far they are reasonable and concordant, and thus to know what may be presumably in error and what may be taken as probable history.

A likely source of confusion is by subsequent compilers taking a gross census of the whole population and applying it to the number of fighting men. This has been done in David's census, where Judah is stated as 500,000 or 470,000 men that drew sword, without Benjamin; whereas in Rehoboam's census Judah and Benjamin were 180,000 men. Clearly Judah did not fall off from 500,000 to less than 180,000 during the prosperous reign of Solomon. We must take, then, the census of David as that of the whole population. This gives the proportion of 18 to 50, less something for Benjamin, or say 1 to 3, for the fighters in the whole population. This means that a man was in the ranks for two-thirds of his life, which implies that those under 15 were about one-third or one-fourth of the whole, a very probable condition.

The starting-point of numbers is complicated by the probable accretion of many broken tribes in Moab, and at other periods. Whenever the Israelites fought there must always have been tribes that would side with them, and join in the attack; owing both to old feuds, and to the universal custom of siding with the victors. Hence we have to do, not only with natural increase, but also with continual accretion through all the fighting period. Even down to the time of David, the Canaanites were continually being incorporated with Israel; Uriah the Hittite was a leading man, the Gibeonites had been absorbed, and the Cherethites, Pelethites, and Gittites were in honour. If we accept the census of 40,000 at the crossing of Jordan as referring to the whole people, it seems a fair basis for the subsequent number (Figs. 27, 28, 29).

The question, then, is what uniform increase is shown by a growth of 40,000 at 1170 B.C. to 1,300,000 by 979 B.C., in 191 years? This means a difference between annual death-rate and birth-rate of 18 per thousand, which in a generation of 25 years means about 3 descendants for each 2 parents. Comparing this with the growth of England early in the last century, we find it to be just the same. But it is far exceeded by the growth of Egypt at present, where the country birth-rate is 60–70 per 1000, and death-rate 30–50. Taking 65 and 40 as the average, the increase is 25 per 1000 annually (or 850 per 1000 in 25 years); 40,000 in 191 years would increase in Egypt, at the present rate, to 4,440,000. There is, then, no reason against accepting the increase as regular, from the 40,000 at Jordan to the numbers under the monarchy, the losses by war being probably more than compensated by the gains of accretion from kindred people. As we can hardly suppose that the Israelites, after largely exterminating the inhabitants, increased

FIG. 27.—Heads of Hittites, from Armenia.
FIG. 28.—Heads of Amorites from Syria. Akin to the North Africans.
FIG. 29.—Philistines. Probably from Crete.

THE PERIOD OF JUDGES

in Canaan slower than England increased during a time of peace, we cannot suppose that the whole population was more than 40,000 at the beginning. The actual statements of high numbers that we have are as follows:

Date.	Record.		Normal growth.	
			All.	Men.
1170?	Jericho (Jos. iv, 13) ...	40,000	(40,000)	(13,000)
1170?	Attack Ai (Jos. viii, 3, 12)	35,000		
	Canaanites slain at Ai, 12,000			
1144	Levy against Midian (Jud. vii, 3)	32,000	64,000	21,000
	Midianites slain, 120,000 (Jud. viii, 10)			
1134	Moabites slain, 10,000 (Jud. iii, 29)			
1090	Naphtali and Zebulon, 10,000 (Jud. iv, 6) ...	∴ 60,000	172,000	57,000
∴ 1057	First-born, 22,273 (Num. iii, 43); × 14 for population	310,000	(310,000)	
∴ 1040	Israel and Benjamin (Jud. xx, 15, 17) ...	426,000	(426,000)	
1030	Israel and Judah (1 Sam. xi, 8)	330,000	510,000	170,000
979	Israel and Judah (2 Sam. xxiv, 9)	1,300,000	(1,300,000)	(430,000)

The numbers in brackets are those copied in from the Record, as termini, or as indicating the date of the first-born dedication, and of the Benjaminite war. The unknown fluctuations due to accretion of allied tribes, or defections in the assembly, prevent any close conclusions being drawn; the earlier numbers seem as if the whole census had been copied as the number of men. And the accretion of eastern tribes must have been very large to bring up the 6000 of the desert census to 40,000. But we have to remember that the policy was to keep all the captive girls, " to every man a damsel or two," after each big fight, so that with polygamy on a large scale the numbers would increase greatly beyond those normal to the number of men. Gideon had 70 sons, Jair had 30, Ibzan had 30, and Abdon had 40.

The general conclusion as to numbers seems to be that there is nothing unlikely in the Record, when we regard the probable normal increase, the prevalence of polygamy owing to captive girls, and the accretions and defections of allied tribes, whose feuds made them join in the slaughters. There is no need to take the numbers as greatly exaggerated or imaginary. The highest number of all, 1,300,000, under the monarchy, implies about 130 to the square mile, which may be compared with 200 per square mile in Switzerland, where the proportion of bare rock may be about the same. In the present under-stocked condition, Palestine contains about half the number.

27. *Egyptian Influence.*

The productions of the Israelites show their memory of Egypt. It is often assumed that the prohibition to make a graven image was as rigidly carried out as it is now in Islam,—the second monotheistic revival of the Semites. The holy of holies of Solomon's temple contained, however, two gigantic cherubim, about 17 feet high, with wings stretched out, 8 feet on either side. The two stood side by side, right across the back of the shrine. The whole

THE PERIOD OF JUDGES

walls were covered with cherubim and palm-trees and flowers. Not only were figures in the holiest place, but in the open court stood the brazen sea on twelve oxen, and figures of lions, oxen, and cherubim covered the portable tanks. In earlier times, Micah had a graven image and a molten image of silver, weighing about six pounds, in his private chapel of Yahveh, served by a Levite, and these, with the ephod and teraphim, were adopted for tribal worship by part of the tribe of Dan until the Captivity. There was neither officially nor privately any objection to the use of images.

On the holiest of all things, the Ark of Yahveh, there were cherubs, one on each end of the mercy-seat, with their wings covering the mercy-seat. This description is like the Egyptian arks of the gods, with figures of Maat, or Truth, at each end, with their wings covering the ark. There would have been no objection to adopting this idea, as Maat was abstract truth, never worshipped as a local goddess, and was retained even by the bigoted Egyptian monotheist, Akhenaten. Such figures over the mercy-seat may even have given the point to the phrases, "Mercy and Truth are met together"; "For Thy mercy and for Thy truth's sake"; "Let not mercy and truth forsake thee"; "By mercy and truth iniquity is purged;" and "Mercy and Truth preserve the king." May not one of the figures have been called "Mercy," and the other "Truth," at least in the popular description of the Ark? (Fig. 30.)

Another Egyptian model is seen in the border of the high priest's robe, which had a golden bell and a pomegranate alternately round the hem. This is the lotus border of flowers and seed-vessels, which the Egyptians often used; only, as the lotus was unknown in Palestine, it was re-named by popular custom, much as the Greeks, in borrowing it, turned it into the palmetto (Fig. 31).

The strong religious protection under which weights and measures were placed, is seen in Leviticus (xix, 35, 36): "Ye shall do no unrighteousness in judgment, in mete-yard, in weight, or in measure. Just balances, just weights, a just ephah, and a just hin, shall ye have." Again, in Proverbs (xi, 1): "A false balance is abomination to the Lord: but a just weight is His delight"; and (xvi, 11): "A just weight and balance are the Lord's: all the weights of the bag are His work." Similarly, in Syria the weights were preserved in the temples, and in Egypt the standards were, in Roman times, in the Serapeum at Alexandria. It seems not improbable that the Jewish standards may have been kept in the Ark under the guardianship of the figures of Truth. We read that the contents of the Ark were a rod, a vase of one omer, and two stones; these might well be used as the standards of length, capacity, and weight. When it is said that weights are of divine work, it is very near the statement that the tables of the law were of divine work. The rod called Aaron's rod must have been fairly long, as it is said to be comparable to a serpent. The vase of manna is stated to have been the measure of an omer. And the two tables of the law were by no means large slabs of stone, for the Ten Commandments would easily be engraved on one stone the size of the hand. Thus

Fig. 30.—Egyptian ark of a god, with figures of Truth spreading their wings over it. The large curved mass is the linen wrapper which covered the ark, and the upper frame is the section of the shrine in which it stood.

Fig. 31.—Border of lotus flowers and seed-vessels. Called by the Israelites "bells and pomegranates."

To face page 62.

whatever connections these objects had with the past history, it would be quite fitting that the rod, the vase, and the stones should have been appealed to as the standards of Yahveh, kept under the wings of the Truth.

CHAPTER V

THE MONARCHY

DURING the four centuries of the Jewish monarchy there were many connections with the neighbouring great power on the south. The earlier of these are with the line of kings who ruled at Tanis or Zoan in the Delta, toward the Jewish frontier. These kings shared the Nile valley with the priest kings at the older capital, Thebes, who maintained a rival line; this was much like the position of the house of Savoy, on the northern frontier, sharing Italy with the pontiffs in the older capital of Rome. Thus the way was paved for a peaceful intercourse with Palestine; Egypt was divided and weak, its kings could not undertake foreign conquests, they lived on the north-east frontier, and they were not sorry to be civil to a rising power which held all Palestine.

28. *Hadad of Edom.*

The first connection was from a political refugee, Hadad king of Edom, who had taken refuge with Pharaoh on the destruction of his kingdom by David

FIG. 32.—Head of King Siamen, from Memphis.

FIG. 33.—Head of King Sheshenq. "Shishak, King of Egypt."

To face page 64.

THE MONARCHY

and Joab (2 Sam. viii, 14). He was but a little child when he fled with his fugitive servants. In course of time he married the sister of Tahpenes the Egyptian queen, and had a son, Genubath, who was brought up in the court. On hearing of the deaths of David and Joab, he desired to return, and was allowed to do so. All this implies probably twenty to thirty years. Hadad grew up while in Egypt; he must have shown capability before he would be married to the queen's sister, and then his son was "among the sons of Pharaoh" (1 Kings xi, 17-22). David died in 977 B.C.; hence the marriage might be about 985, and the flight to Egypt about 1005 B.C. or earlier. On referring to the history of the Tanite dynasty, it seems that Hadad must have been received by Siamen (Fig. 32); he lived through the obscure reign which followed, and was probably married early in the reign of Pasebkhanu II, who came to the throne in 987; and he continued on to the rise of Shishak—the Egyptian Sheshenq—in 952 B.C. (Fig. 33). Unfortunately we know so little about this period that the queen's name is not preserved, and there is very little remaining of Pasebkhanu.

FIG. 34.—Bead of King Pasebkhanu.

His name was seen by Wilkinson in a tomb at Thebes, now lost; it occurs on a statue, which we shall refer to, in the British Museum; and a bead with the name is here figured (Fig. 34).

29. *Pharaoh's Daughter.*

The next connection is an important one. Solomon had the honour of including a daughter of Pharaoh as a principal wife in his palace. That the Tanite kings should thus mix with the Syrians of Edom and of Judaea is not surprising. Living on the north-east of the Delta, they were sensitive to the frontier politics, and by giving wives to the kings of Syria, they could hope to retain them as allies, or at least to restrain any opposition on their part. We see in the contemporary records of the Old Testament how each ruler had generally many dozen children; and if half a dozen daughters of inferior rank could keep the borders quiet, peace was cheaply purchased. There was thus a great political value in the polygamy of rulers, by supplying hostages and political agents under ties of the strongest personal claims.

The date of this marriage was during the building of the temple, as "Solomon made affinity with Pharaoh, King of Egypt, and took Pharaoh's daughter, and brought her into the city of David, until he had made an end of building his own house and the house of Yahveh" (1 Kings iii, 1). As his accession was in 977, the temple was being built from 974–967, and his palace from 967–955 B.C. Hence the marriage was about 970, and the birth of the princess would have been about 990 B.C. We may note in passing that a lunar reckoning seems to have prevailed then, as the temple was built between the 50th and 140th months of the reign.

An Egyptian princess, born about 990 B.C., must

have been a daughter of king Pasebkhanu II, who reigned from 987–952 B.C., as she was "Pharaoh's daughter" at about 970 B.C. Hence follow some interesting relationships, as we shall see further on. Her requirements seem to have been rather exacting in the Judaean court. "Solomon made also a house for Pharaoh's daughter, whom he had taken, like unto the porch. All these were of costly stones, according to the measures of hewn stones, sawed with saws, within and without, even from the foundation unto the coping" (1 Kings vii, 8, 9). But a decent dowry had been given with the princess, at the cost of the neighbours, "for Pharaoh, King of Egypt, had gone up, and taken Gezer and burnt it with fire, and slain the Canaanites that dwelt in the city, and given it for a present unto his daughter, Solomon's wife. And Solomon built Gezer" (1 Kings ix, 16, 17). These Canaanites had got the upper hand since the time of the conquest, when "they drove not out the Canaanites that dwelt in Gezer; but the Canaanites dwell among the Ephraimites unto this day, and serve under tribute" (Josh. xvi, 10; Jud. i, 29). These references casually show how parts of the text of Joshua and Judges were in shape before the extermination of the Canaanites at 970 B.C., and the subsequent grant of it as a Levitical city (Josh. xxi, 21), which it continued to be till Roman times. When the palace was finished, then "Pharaoh's daughter came up out of the city of David unto her house which Solomon had built for her" (1 Kings ix, 24).

30. Family Links of Egypt and Judah.

We now turn to the family connections resulting from the Egyptian marriage. The known relationships are as below; the birth-years precede the names, where known; the years of reign are below the names. It should be remembered that these connections do not depend on the general exactness of Egyptian or Jewish chronology, but are closely fixed by the war of Shishak with Rehoboam, and the recorded length of reign of Shishak's predecessor.

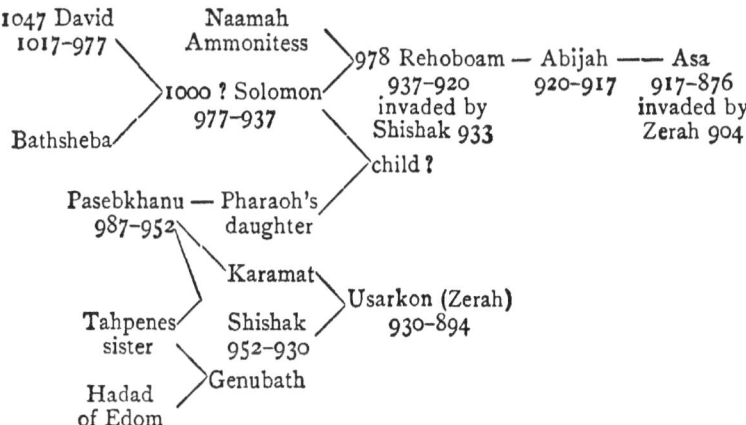

We see, then, how much light family questions can throw on the politics of the time; much as in our own day Bismarck said that every politician ought to have the *Almanach de Gotha* by heart. Shishak's queen, Karamat, was the central figure. Karamat's sister sat on the throne of Judaea with Solomon; Karamat's aunt was queen of the barbarous Edomites, with her Egyptian-bred husband Hadad; Karamat's husband was heir to Egypt, and when her sister's

husband, Solomon, died, he intervened and over-ran
Judaea, probably in the name of his nephew, the child
of Pharaoh's daughter; lastly, it was Karamat's son
who again invaded Judaea, but found the task too

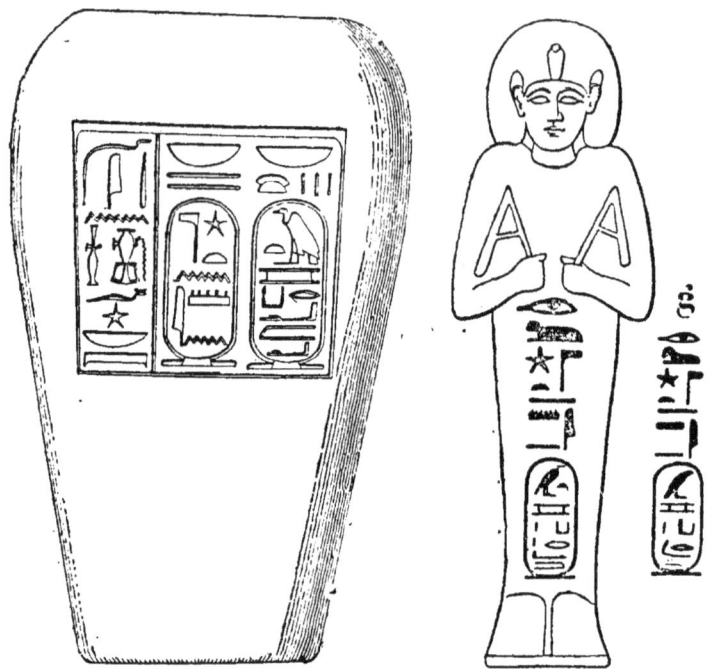

FIG. 35.—Canopic jar and ushabti of Queen Karamat.

hard for him, in the days of Asa. It is an interesting
fact that the tomb of this central figure, queen
Karamat, was known to the natives at Thebes about
1840, but is now lost to sight. From it came her
funeral vases now in Berlin, and her funeral figures of
servants in Berlin, Paris, and Philadelphia (Fig. 35).

31. *Shechem the Old Centre.*

To realise the meaning of the next act, we must look back into the earlier history. Shechem had been the old Patriarchal centre; the traditions of the race clung to the mountains of Ephraim. Abram had first settled at Shechem from Haran; Jacob, when he returned from Aram had centred there, and Jacob's well was venerated through the ages. There Joshua had built the altar for the great oath of the tribes, of blessing and cursing, when the law was read to them—six tribes on Gerizim to bless, and six tribes on Ebal to curse. A few miles to the south, on the same ridge, was Shiloh, where the centre of national worship was fixed during the time of the Judges (Josh. xviii, 1; 1 Sam. i, 3). Even long after that, Ezekiel portioned out in vision a new allotment of the land, in which the Divine centre was to fall on Shechem, and not on Jerusalem. As the woman of Samaria said, "Our father Jacob gave us the well and drank thereof. . . . Our fathers worshipped in this mountain." And to this day the venerable survival of the worship, that has lasted unbroken for three thousand years, may be seen in its original centre.

32. *The Israelite View.*

Let us now look at the position as it must have appealed to an Israelite of those times. What was the upstart pretension of Benjamin and Judah to rival the ancient shrines of Ephraim? Because Saul was of Benjamin, and David of Judah, were they to have a rival sanctuary? Was the newly captured fortress of the Jebusites to supplant the rightful centres of worship? For Hebron much might have been pleaded, but for Jerusalem no Israelite could have any veneration. David might hold it with his outlandish Cherethites and Pelethites, Solomon might grind them with taxes and labour for his heathenish buildings, after the manner of Egypt, with his altar of hewn stones, and his crowds of cherubs and lions and ornaments all over the work. But the patriotism of Israel longed for the ancient sanctuaries of Ephraim.

Abiyah, the prophet of Shiloh, jealous for its ancient glories, looked to the deputy of the king, who was over all Ephraim and Manasseh. He was a mighty man of valour, and industrious in civil affairs. Here was one whose zeal had rendered him popular in the ancient centres, and who was well fitted to rule. Jeroboam was the needful man. The prophet waylaid him as he returned to his charge, when they were alone in the country, and, rending his garment, gave him ten pieces, and left but two to represent the share of Jerusalem. The king heard of it, and there was no safety for any man with such a prediction upon him; so "Jeroboam arose and fled into Egypt, unto Shishak, King of Egypt, and was in Egypt until the death of Solomon."

The new reign began. Rehoboam felt the weakness of the claim of Jerusalem as a centre for the tribes, and he had to go to Shechem, because all Israel gathered there to make him king. But before accepting Rehoboam, they sent for their old ruler, Jeroboam, out of Egypt. He was to be the national spokesman to the headstrong son of Solomon. The breach was soon irrevocable; and even the priestly writers of Jerusalem said that "Yahveh spake by

Ahiyah of Shiloh unto Jeroboam the son of Nebat" (1 Kings xii, 15), and a prophet of Jerusalem forbad Rehoboam to think of revenge.

Jeroboam then rebuilt Shechem in Mount Ephraim, dear to all the associations of the people. He set up again the golden calf, which had been worshipped in the wilderness as the God which brought Israel up out of Egypt, and which Solomon had debased to bear his brazen sea. The old "house of God," Beth-El, was to be the holy centre on the southern border, as ·Dan was to be in the north. Ephraim envied Judah, and Judah vexed Ephraim.

33. *Shishak's Invasion.*

Judah being thus reduced to a mere fragment of its former power, it could not resist Egypt. Shishak had started a new and vigorous dynasty on the eastern border of the Delta. Jeroboam was his friend, and Judah was therefore his enemy. Moreover, there was apparently a serious ground of complaint. Solomon had probably some issue by Shishak's sister-in-law; but the royal descent from Egypt was slighted, and a son of a backwoods Ammonitess was given the kingdom. This was ample ground for a military promenade round the land of Judah, to eat up all the produce, and strip it of the treasure which his wealthy brother-in-law had accumulated. "And he took away the treasures of the house of Yahveh, and the treasures of the king's house; he even took away all." The army consisted of 1200 chariots and 60,000 horsemen, and people without number, Lubim and Sukkim and Cushim.

Fig. 36.—Figure of the god Amon holding captive the cities of Judah for Shishak.
Fig. 37.—One of the heads of the cities, Jud-ha-malek (Jehud of the king, Josh. xix, 45), which is the third behind the knee of the god Amon.

THE MONARCHY 73

These are the different divisions of the Egyptian army—west, east, and south. The Lubim are the Libyans; the Sukkim the dwellers in the land of Succoth, or booths of the Wady Tumilat; and the Cushim the Sudani troops. The identification of the Sukkim is certain, because the same forms of "s" and "k" are used as in Succoth, so that the words might be more precisely written "Cukkim" and "Cukkoth."

This campaign seems to have been near the end of Shishak's reign. It is represented outside the south wall of the great forecourt at Karnak; and the quarry of stone at Silsileh has an inscription, naming the work for this court, and dated in the twenty-first year. From the Jewish and Assyrian chronology, the fifth year of Rehoboam, in which the invasion took place, was in 933 B.C.; and if we count the twentieth year of Shishak as equal to that, it agrees very well with all the other facts of Egyptian chronology.

The result of the campaign is shown at Karnak, by a gigantic figure of Amon, the god of Thebes, leading captive all the cities of Judah. They are designated by name-labels, each headed by the bust of a captive, and Amon is presenting them to Shishak. Unfortunately, the work, begun just at the close of the reign, was never completed, and the figure of the conqueror has not been carved (Figs. 36, 37).

The names begin with some general names of countries, and then some names in the north of Palestine, but after the first two dozen, they continue steadily within Judaea. Had it not been for some unhappy destructions, we should have had over a hundred names of Jewish towns. As it is, about a quarter of them have been identified. They are mostly in the fertile slopes of the western side of the land, but some are along the hills overlooking the Dead Sea. They are so uniformly scattered over a large part of the country that, if actually visited by the army of Shishak, the clearance of the wealth of the land must have been very thorough. It may be, however, that some of the tribute lists of Solomon, such as the list of the 250 officers "that bare rule over the people," may have been taken and copied, as showing the capture of the kingdom.

34. *Usarkon's Invasion.*

The next connection with Egypt is the invasion by Zerakh, shortly before the 15th year of Asa (2 Chron. xv, 10), that is, before 903 B.C. This falls in the reign of Usarkon I, 930–894 B.C., and the name Zerah—or Zerakh as it actually is—gives a very likely corruption of the Egyptian's name (Fig. 38). We read (2 Chron. xiv, 9), "There came out against them (the army of Asa) Zerakh the Ethiopian with an host of a million (men) and three hundred chariots; and came unto Mareshah. Then Asa went out against him. . . . So Yahveh smote the Ethiopians before Asa and before Judah; and the Ethiopians fled.

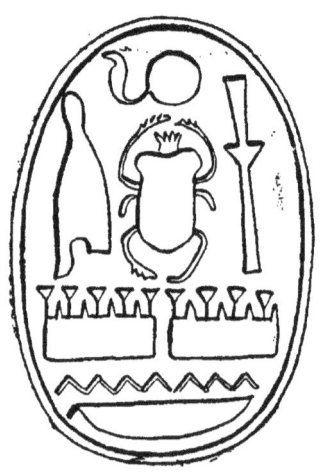

FIG. 38.—Scarab of Shishak with the united name of Usarkon (Zerah).

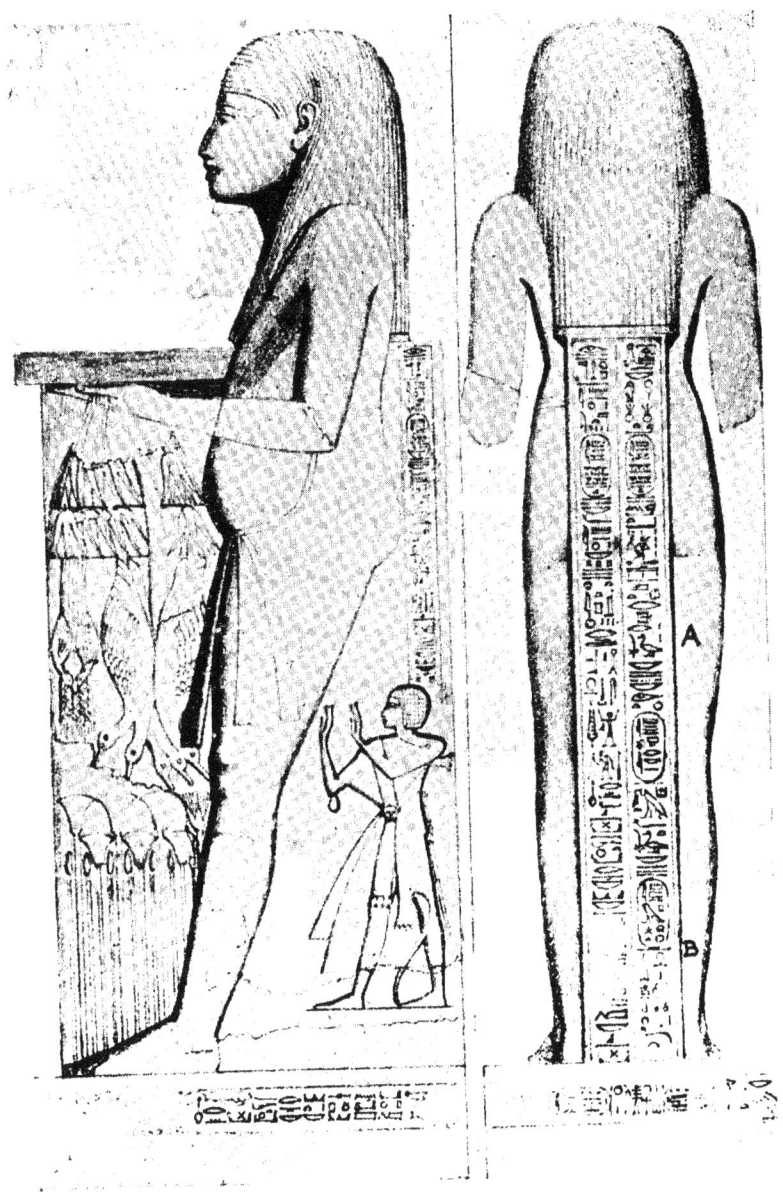

FIG. 39.—Figure of the Nile god. Down the back from A to B is the important mention of "the king's son, Usarkon (Zerah), whose mother was Karamat, daughter of King Pasebkhanu," the sister-in-law of Solomon.

THE MONARCHY 75

And Asa and the people that were with him pursued them unto Gerar; and the Ethiopians were overthrown, that they could not recover themselves; for they were broken before Yahveh and before His host; and they carried away very much spoil. And they smote all the cities round about Gerar." An attempt has been made to deny the Egyptian connection, and refer this to some unknown king of an unknown people. But the name agrees to the known king of the time in Egypt; the army was composed of Libyans and Sudanis (2 Chron. xvi, 8), which could only come from Egypt; and they fled to Gerar on the way to Egypt in their return. This king had a son Shishak, who dedicated a large statue of the Nile (Hapi), on which he recorded his father's descent from Karamat and Pasebkhanu. This precious figure, now in the British Museum, gives us the historical basis of this family (Fig. 39).

35. *Shabaka, the Viceroy.*

After nearly two centuries Egypt began to assert its power again. The latter part of the twenty-second dynasty, after Usarkon, had been a time of decline, and the twenty-third dynasty was very weak. The Ethiopian rulers pushed northward, Pankhy conquering the whole of Egypt about 750 B.C., and Kashta—who apparently was his son—succeeding from 725 to 715 B.C. But a realm of such great extent, stretching from the capital at Napata in Ethiopia to the frontier, as far as from France to the Bosphorus, could hardly be controlled by a single ruler, when about three miles an hour was the quickest rate of communication.

Accordingly the heir apparent was sent to govern Egypt as a viceroy, who was almost independent. This system is shown by Sargon of Assyria terming Shabaka "the Tartan of Muzri," or commander-in-chief of Egypt at 720 B.C. in the reign of Kashta; and later on Taharqa was sent down north at twenty years old, as he informs us, while he did not come to the throne till he was twenty-nine. Were it not for the British occupation of Egypt, that land would now be similarly governed from Omdurman by the Sudanis. This system explains the fact of the reigns of Shabaka and Tirhakah coming a few years later than the dates at which they appear in Jewish history.

Not only Judah, but the more distant Israel, began to be dominated by the Ethiopian power. "Hoshea had sent messengers to Sua, King of Egypt, and brought no present to the King of Assyria, as he had done year by year" (2 Kings xvii, 4). The name rendered as So in the A.V. is actually Sua in the Hebrew; and from the two forms of the similar name, Bathshua and Bathsheba, we see that Sua is equal to Seba. The Assyrian record has the form Sibe the Tartan of Muzri, which is clearly the same. In Egyptian the name is Shabaka, meaning the wild cat; in modern Nubian the male wild cat is *sab*, and *ki* is the article put after it. This article is omitted in common use, as is seen in the name of the island Pila*k*, which became Philae; and as also in Arabic names the article is often dropped by foreigners, *e.g.* Cairo for El Kahira. Thus there is no difficulty in the stages of degradation of the name from Shabaka to Shaba, Saba, Seba, Sua, and, worst of all in English, So (Fig. 40).

Fig. 40.—Head of Shabaka. "So, King of Egypt."

Fig. 41.—Head of Tabarqa. "Tirhakah, King of Ethiopia"

To face page 76.

THE MONARCHY 77

It seems that Egypt was retaining a hold upon the south of Palestine. When Zerakh was defeated and fled, Asa spoiled all the cities round about Gerar near Gaza as Egyptian possessions. When Sargon pushed on, after the capture of Samaria in 722 B C., he attacked in 720 Hanun of Gaza and Sibe of Muzri, implying that there were Egyptian possessions close to Gaza. In 715 Rabshakeh reproached Hezekiah, "Thou trustest upon the staff of this bruised reed, upon Egypt; whereon if a man lean, it will go into his hand, and pierce it; so is Pharaoh King of Egypt unto all that trust on him."

36. *Tirhakah, the Ethiopian.*

The next link is the campaign of Sennacherib in Judaea, in 701 B.C., where Taharqa (Tirhakah) is named as being King of Ethiopia, and Hezekiah was warned against trusting to him. Taharqa was not sole sovereign till 693 at the death of Shabatoka; but he had been sent down to Egypt at the age of twenty as viceroy. The Jewish writers did not distinguish between viceroys of Egypt and sole kings, either in Sua or Tirhakah, but the Assyrians used the term commander-in-chief correctly (Fig. 41).

On the base which remains at Karnak, built for a statue of Taharqa, there is a long list of conquered towns, which comprises much of Palestine. But there is no evidence of his actually occupying Palestine. The list proves to have been copied name for name from the list of Sety I. Again, there is a list of cities on a statuette of Taharqa; and once more we can detect it to be a mere copy from a list on the colossus of Rameses II. Egypt does not seem to have secured at the utmost more than a frontier border in Syria.

37. *Expeditions of Necho.*

After some three generations of the dominance of Babylonia, Egypt once more spread its power. A border claim had always been kept up. Psamtek had from 624 to 596 held the south of Palestine up to Ashdod, where he barred the great Scythian invasion from spreading over into Egypt. He thus held for Egypt, Ashkelon, Gaza and Gerar, which had been frontier cities of old.

Once more Egypt re-asserted its old claims in a spasmodic way. Pharaoh·Necho King of Egypt in 609 B.C. came up to fight the King of Assyria at Carchemish by the Euphrates, and Josiah went out against him. But he sent ambassadors to him saying, "What have I to do with thee, thou King of Judah? I come not against thee this day, but against the house wherewith I have war; for God commanded me to make haste; forbear thee from God who is with me, that He destroy thee not. Nevertheless, Josiah would not turn his face from him, but disguised himself that he might fight with him, and hearkened not unto the words of Necho from the mouth of God, and came to fight in the valley of Megiddo. And the archers shot at King Josiah; and the king said to his servants, Have me away, for I am sore wounded. His servants therefore took him out of that chariot, and put him in the second chariot that he had, and carried him dead from Megiddo, and brought him to Jerusalem, and buried him in his own sepulchre"

(2 Kings xxiii, 29, 30; 2 Chron. xxxv, 20–24). Necho went on and took Kadesh, and advanced to the Euphrates. But this was only a raid, and in three months he was back again in Northern Palestine at Riblah, and there deposed Jehoahaz who had succeeded Josiah, and set up as king Eliakim the son

Fig. 42.—Triumphal scarab of Necho.

of Josiah, and called him Jehoiakim. Jehoahaz was taken captive to Egypt and died there. Necho tried to hold Syria, and four years later, in 605 B.C., he again struck out to the Euphrates at Carchemish, but he was crushed by Nebuchadrezzar, and Egypt never again touched its old limits (Jer. xlvi, 2) (Fig. 42).

Another Egyptian expedition must have taken place between 598 and 588 B.C., probably about 597.

A Chaldean army was besieging Jerusalem, and an Egyptian army came up and drove them away. But on the Egyptians leaving, the Chaldeans returned (Jer. xxxvii, 5–8). Yet again in 594, probably on the accession of Psamtek II, Zedekiah broke faith with Nebuchadrezzar, and "rebelled against him in sending his ambassadors into Egypt, that they might give him horses and much people" (Ezek. xvii, 15); and in 589 and 588 Ezekiel uttered long denunciations against Egypt (xxix to xxxii). Thus Judaea was entangled in the Egyptian politics down to the end of the monarchy, till that terrible day when "the famine prevailed in the city, and there was no bread for the people. And the city was broken up, and all the men of war fled by night."

CHAPTER VI

THE CAPTIVITY

38. *The Three Captivities.*

THE Captivity is generally considered to have begun at the final fall of Jerusalem; but Jeremiah distinguishes the three captivities, of which the first was the greater. In the 7th or 8th year of Nebuchadrezzar, 598 B.C., the Babylonian army took Jerusalem, removed all the gold work that was left in the temple, "all the treasures of the house of Yahveh, and the treasures of the king's house, and cut in pieces all the vessels of gold which Solomon had made in the temple of Yahveh." The royal family, all the chief people, all craftsmen and smiths were taken, 3023 in number. Only the poorest people remained, to be ruled by a king set up by the Babylonians. It was in this great captivity that Ezekiel was deported to the river Chebar; his 30th year that he begins to date by, is the era of Nabopolassar continued into the reign of his son. The years of Nebuchadrezzar are fixed in Jewish reigns by Jer. xxv, 1.

The next captivity ensued on the final taking of Jerusalem in the 19th year of Nebuchadrezzar,

588 B.C., after a siege of eighteen months. The remaining men of the royal family were all deported or slain, and the city ceased to be a stronghold. The next stage was in the following month when all the walls were broken down, all the buildings burnt, and all the bronze broken and carried away as spoil— a complete gutting and destruction. This time, 832 captives were removed.

The last captivity was after the rebellion, and slaughter of Gedaliah, the governor left by the Babylonians, when in the 23rd year of Nebuchadrezzar, 584 B.C., a final deportation of 745 captives took place (Jer. lii, 28-30).

39. *Permanence of the Population.*

The question naturally arises, how much of the population of the lower classes was left? We have seen that the numbers at the beginning of the monarchy were 1,300,000. Supposing that they were largely reduced by misgovernment, wars, and famines, we could hardly put them at less than a fifth, say 150,000 for Israel and 100,000 for Judah, at the least. Now 27,290 people are stated by Sargon to have been removed from Israel, or only a sixth of the whole, leaving therefore five-sixths in the country. Of Judah a total of 4600 captives was taken, as stated by the apparently exact record of Jeremiah (Jer. lii, 30), or only one-thirtieth of the whole. Even if the larger estimate of 10,000 is adopted, we cannot suppose in view of these numbers that the whole captivities did more than remove a small fraction of the population. That fraction was what gave unity,

THE CAPTIVITY 83

government, nationality, and character to the Jewish people. The upper class scribes who were removed looked on all the rest as dross, "this people who knoweth not the law are cursed"; the country-man, who still worshipped the queen of heaven, was contemptuously disregarded by them at the return. But so far as descent goes, the population of Palestine remained practically the same in Roman times as it had been under Solomon.

How much was Jewish throughout is another question. The Canaanite was not driven out from the greater part of the land, and he naturally mixed with the Jew in a few centuries. As Ezekiel said to Jerusalem: "Thy birth and thy nativity is of the land of Canaan; thy father was an Amorite and thy mother a Hittite. . . . Your mother was a Hittite and your father an Amorite. And thine elder sister is Samaria, she and her daughters that dwell at thy left hand; and thy younger sister that dwelleth at thy right hand is Sodom and her daughters" (Ezek. xvi, 3, 46). The portraiture of the heads of Jewish towns under Shishak is the usual Syrian and Amorite type. The race may have been very mixed under the monarchy; but what it was then it continued to be as a whole, at least down to Roman times.

Though in Jeremiah there is an apparently exact count of 4600 as the total of captives, there is a higher statement in 2 Kings xxiv, 14, of 10,000 for the first captivity, in place of 3023. Now, 10,000 seems a round guess; but two verses later the detail of 7000 soldiers and 1000 artisans is stated, which can hardly be reduced to the 3023 of Jeremiah. It seems most likely that, as the active men were about a third of the population in earlier accounts, so here 3023 was the number of men, and 10,000 the total people. If so, the total of 4600 in the three captivities would imply 15,000 total people. This might be a tenth of a much-reduced population, but we cannot suppose it to represent even a considerable share of the whole.

Under Nehemiah the return is stated to be altogether 42,360 and 7337 servants. But the totals of the separate items are only 31,629, and the 1 in 10 that went to Jerusalem are 3044, implying 30,440 for the whole. If 15,000 went into captivity, in 63 years' increase in Babylonia they might amount to 65,000 if they increased like modern Egyptians. So only half of their descendants would suffice to account for the number that returned.

40. *The Refugees in Egypt.*

We now turn to the Egyptian connections during the Captivity. The Babylonian had in 599 B.C. tried a king of his own choice, but without success, the rebellion of 589 being the result; he now named a governor directly responsible to the king at Babylon. But the new governor Gedaliah, the grandson of the chief scribe of Josiah, was soon assassinated by a descendant of the kings, named Ishmael, who hoped to profit by the change. Knowing that such contempt would be avenged, the more sober party felt that they dare not stay, and so went down into Egypt, after rescuing the king's daughters and principal people.

"Johanan the son of Kareah, and all the captains

THE CAPTIVITY

of the forces, took all the remnant of Judah, that were returned from all nations, whither they had been driven, to dwell in the land of Judah; even men, women and children, and the king's daughters, and every person that Nabuzar-adan the captain of the guard had left with Gedaliah, and Jeremiah the prophet, and Baruch the son of Neriah. So they came into the land of Egypt, even to Tahpanhes" (Jer. xliii, 5-7). This same city is referred to as a garrison of Egypt. "The children of Noph and Tahapanes have broken the crown of thy head" (Jer. ii, 16). Noph is colloquial for Men-nofer, Menfi, Memphis. Again, "publish in Migdol, and publish in Noph and Tahpanhes" (Jer. xlvi, 14). In the list of chief places of Egypt it also occurs. " I will make Pathros desolate (Pa-ta-res, 'the south land'), and will set fire in Zoan (Tanis), and will execute judgments in No (Nia, Assyrian for Thebes). And I will pour out My fury on Sin (Pelusium). . . . No shall be rent asunder, and Noph (Memphis) shall have distresses daily. The young men of Aven (On, Heliopolis) and of Pi-beseth (Bubastis, 'city of Bast') shall fall by the sword. . . . At Tehaphnehes also the day shall be darkened, when I shall break there the yokes of Egypt" (Ezek. xxx, 14-18).

41. *Position of Tehaphnehes.*

These references show that Tehaphnehes was an important garrison, and as the Jews fled there it must have been close to the frontier. It is thus clear that it was the Greek Daphnae, the modern Tell Defneh, which is on the road to Palestine. The extreme frontier city of Pelusium was to the north of the caravan road; but Daphnae was the first fortress on that road, which touched the river and canal system of the Delta. For all travelling and commercial purposes it was the frontier of Egypt; east of it there was desert for 150 miles, till the gardens of Gaza came in sight.

The main importance of Daphnae began when there was an Asiatic power sufficiently organised to be able to throw an army across the week's journey of desert. Ever since the invasion of the barbarous Hyksos, there had been no danger to Egypt from the Syrian side, until the rise of Assyrian power. Tiglath Pileser III had induced some border region to receive a resident of his, perhaps in Sinai or the isthmus, about 740 B.C. Sargon in 720 had driven back the outposts of Shabaka, near Gaza. The blow came when Esarhaddon, in 670 B.C., cleared the desert tribes out of the way, and reached the Wady Tumilat; swiftly in three weeks he was master of Memphis, then laid a tribute on the Delta, and returned. The Delta chiefs thought it safer to acknowledge him rather than Tirhakah, who came back to Memphis and tried to re-assert himself. Next year Esarhaddon set out, but died by the way. After his death Asshur-bani-pal continued the campaign, and finally cleared the Nile valley up to Thebes, which was sacked. This almost ended the power of Ethiopia in the north; a few years of precarious trouble finished it.

The way was thus open for the strongest of the Delta chiefs to rise. For nearly a century, a line of princes had been claiming sovereign rights in their

Libyan settlement on the west of the Delta. When the Ethiopian was disposed of, the sturdy Psamtek—"the lion's son," as his name means—who had come to the throne as a young man of about twenty-five, steadily gained in power until he held all Egypt in his dominion, and died an old man of eighty.

42. *Importance of Tehaphnehes.*

We are now in a position to understand the politics of the time, and the importance of Daphnae. The Assyrian was the most dangerous power, though the Ethiopian might also cause trouble. Psamtek had acquired his power over the other chiefs by using the Greek mercenaries, the Karlans and Ionians. They could not be assimilated with the Egyptians, but they were invaluable as frontier defenders. So they were settled "at the Pelusian Daphnae against the Arabians and Syrians," as Herodotos says. Psamtek built a strong fortress at this last watering station on the caravan road to Syria. A square pile of brickwork, 143 feet wide, formed a basis, probably 30 or 40 feet high, for the fortress. From the top of that, a far watch over the desert plains could be maintained. To the block was added another on the north-east for royal quarters, and on the south were the store-rooms. The whole stood in a great fortified camp, having a wall over 40 feet thick. This formed the Greek breakwater against any invasion from Asia (Fig. 43).

The importance of such a centre in relation to Jewish life must be taken into account. From the middle of the reign of Manasseh, through the time of

Amon, Josiah, Jehoiakim, and Zedekiah, on into the anarchy after the destruction of Jerusalem, the one place of safety across the border was the Greek garrison. The Jew was a trader anciently as now; that is seen by the Aswan papyri. No doubt he brought the wares of Syria across to the mercenaries, who had come from rocky Karia, and who must have been sick of dulness on a flat sandy desert. Their colony of strange women, picked up in their adventures, and Levantine riff-raff of followers, must have also welcomed any new thing brought by the camel caravan across that forbidding desert, which cut them off from the north. Whenever there was trouble at home, the Jewish noble could escape it at the fortress of Daphnae; whenever there was profit abroad, the Jewish trader could find it nearest in the garrison of Daphnae. For three generations before the end of the monarchy, the Greeks must have been familiar to the more enterprising of the Jews; and probably many a *kaithros*, *psanterin*, and *sumphonyah*, as they called the Greek musical instruments, had been traded over to Jerusalem from the Greek colony, and were well known before we find them in the Jewish literature (Fig. 45).

It was, then, the most natural thing that when a party were in fear of the vengeance of the Assyrians, they should all betake them to the safety of the Greek garrison over the border. As the king's daughters were with the party of Johanan, doubtless they would appeal to the King of Egypt for some help. Haaabra (Apries, Hophra) had recently come to the throne in 589, and one of his first acts had been to try to hold the south of Palestine in alliance with

FIG. 43.—Restoration of the fortress of Tehaphnehes, or Defeneh. The entry is seen at the inner angle, and the pavement of brickwork before it.

FIG. 44.—Pottery oven for baking the Paschal lamb, at the base of the mound of the city of Oniah.

THE CAPTIVITY

Judah. From that the Babylonians had beaten him off, when they destroyed Jerusalem in 588. So, to a fugitive royal party from there, he might be expected to show friendship and good will. There were doubtless some state apartments in the fortress for the Egyptian governors who might visit there. Those

FIG. 45.—Greek vase with hares, from Tehaphnehes.

might be at the disposal of the royal daughters, and Johanan and the men of might would strengthen the camp. Of this an echo comes across the long ages; the fortress mound is known as the Qasr Bint el Yehudi, the palace of the Jew's daughter. It is named *Qasr*, a palace, not *Qala*, a fortress. It is not named Tell Bint el Yehudi, as it would be if it were called so after it were a ruinous heap. *Qasr* is a name which shows its descent from the time of habitation, and habitation for nobility and not merely for troops. So through the long ages of Greek and Roman and Arab there has come down the memory of the royal residence of the king's daughters from the wreck of Jerusalem.

43. *The Babylonianizing Party.*

Jeremiah was by no means satisfied with this flight into Egypt. He had always belonged to the Babylonian party as against the Egyptian alliance. As early as 609 B.C. he had prophesied that all lands were to be given into the hand of Nebuchadrezzar (Jer. xxvii, 8), and he had been protected by Ahikam, the son of Shaphan, who was formerly the chief scribe of Josiah (2 Kings xxii, 3 ; Jer. xxvi, 24). This combination of interests continued. In 607 Jeremiah prophesied the captivity for seventy years (Jer. xxv, 11 ; xxix, 10). In 606 Baruch read the roll of prophecies of Jeremiah in the chamber of Gemariah, son of Shaphan (Jer. xxxvi, 10), probably the resort of the party. After the first and greatest captivity in 598, Jeremiah wrote to the captives that they should settle and prosper as much as possible in Babylonia (Jer. xxix, 5-7). In 596 he prophesied that all the rest of the vessels and brass should be taken by the Babylonians (Jer. xxvii, 19-22). In 591 he declared that Jerusalem was given to the Babylonians (Jer. xxxiv, 2) ; and the next year declared that the city would be taken (Jer. xxxii, 3). In 589, when the Egyptian army was present, and the Babylonian

siege was raised, Jeremiah yet persisted that the
Egyptians would go back, and that in any case the
Babylonians would take the city (Jer. xxxvii, 7–10);
and he tried to persuade Zedekiah and all the people
to go and deliver themselves up (Jer. xxxviii, 2, 17).
When at last the city fell, this advocate of Babylon
was not neglected, but amid all the confusion and
rapine, the captain of the guard found time to send
and fetch Jeremiah out of prison, and gave him in
charge of Gedaliah, son of his old friend Ahikam,
who was already trusted as a Babylonian agent.
Taken with the captives to Ramah, he was there
liberated, and advised to go back and join the
government of Gedaliah, who was now the representative of Babylon (Jer. xxxix, 14; xl, 1, 6). Thus
for twenty years there had been a Babylonianizing
party, of which the descendants of the chief scribe
Shaphan were the agents, and Jeremiah was the
spokesman.

44. *The Prophecy of Jeremiah.*

After such a long antagonism to Egypt, it must
have been bitter to Jeremiah to be taken there, and
to have to depend on Egypt for his bread. He persisted that however safe their position seemed in
Egypt, yet even there Nebuchadrezzar would reach
them. His message to the Jews in Egypt was, "Take
great stones in thine hand, and hide them in the clay
of the pavement which is at the entry of Pharaoh's
house in Tahpanhes, in the sight of the men of Judah;
and say unto them, Thus saith Yahveh of hosts,
the God of Israel; Behold, I will send and take

Nebuchadrezzar the King of Babylon, My servant, and will set his throne upon these stones that I have hid; and he shall spread his royal pavilion over them. And when he cometh, he shall smite the land of Egypt" (Jer. xliii, 9-11; xlvi, 13) (Fig. 46).

The term here "pavement" was rendered in the old A.V. "brick-kiln," and in the R.V. "brickwork or pavement." It means a place of bricks, or a space paved over with bricks. Not being accustomed to such an idea, the translators could not see the sense of it. But when I came to clear the fort at Defneh, there proved to be but one entry into Pharaoh's house; and in front of that was a wide paved area on the north of the fort. It was a place probably for the external guard, and for stacking goods, unloading camels, and such purposes of out-door life in Egypt. Much of it had been washed away in the rains, and there were no stones in the part that was left. The denudation by rain and wind is extreme along the coast, as is seen by the great wall of the camp, forty feet thick, which was so completely swept away that there was no trace visible, and it could only be found beneath the surface. This platform, however, was a place exactly corresponding to Jeremiah's detailed account, and the identification of it is certain.

45. *The Fate of Hophra.*

Jeremiah also prophesied that Pharaoh Hophra should be given into the hand of his enemies, and into the hand of them that seek his life (Jer. xliv, 30). This was remarkably true, for in 570 Aahmes rebelled, on behalf of the Egyptians, against Hophra and his

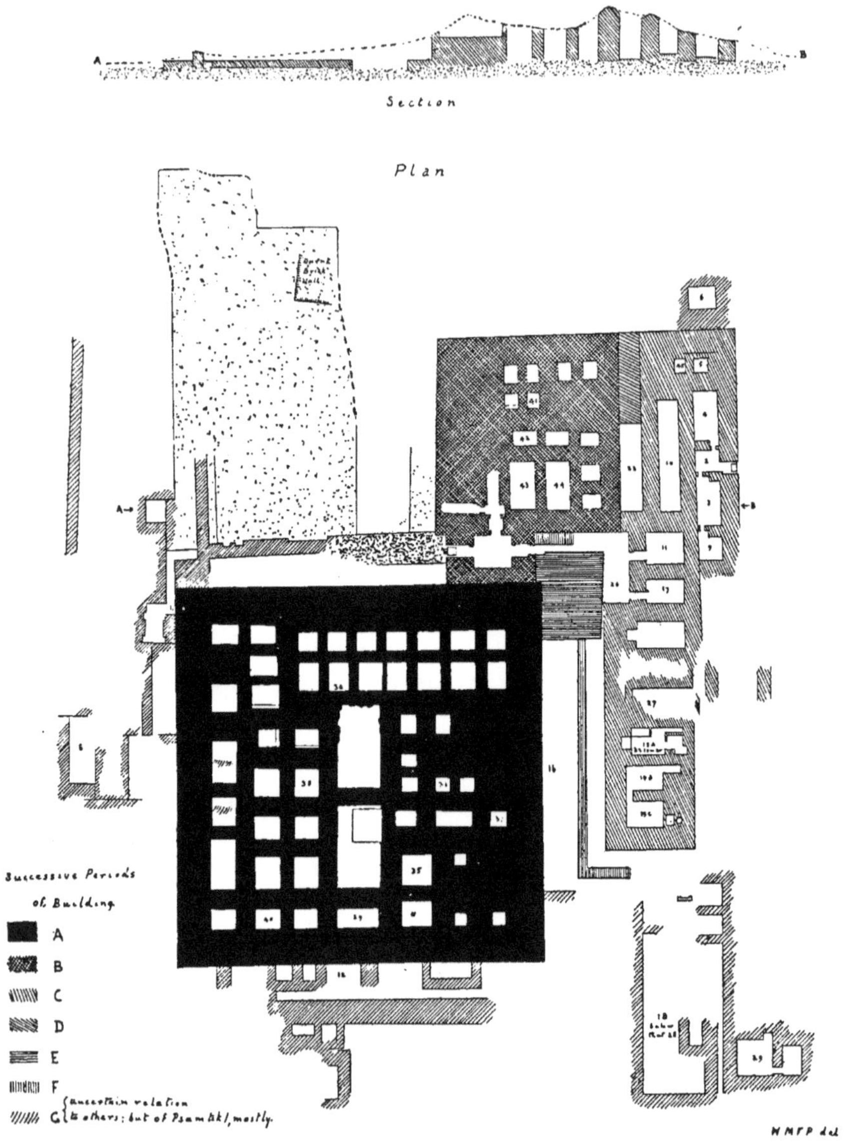

FIG. 46.—Plan of the fort of Tehaphnehes, with the various periods of building marked by different shading.

To face page 92.

Greek party. He reduced Hophra to captivity, nominally a joint rule. After three years Hophra escaped, and began to rally the Greeks, and to settle them along the west of the Delta. Six months later he was defeated by Aahmes, and strangled by them that sought his life. It may be noted that the Hebrew form Hophra is very close to the Egyptian Haa-ab-ra, which was pronounced Hoavra,—what we write as *b* being sounded as *v*, then and later. The Greek form Apries is much less exact.

The effect of this triumph of Aahmes and the Egyptians over the Greek troops, was that the Greeks were expelled from all Egypt, except one treaty port of Naukratis. Daphnae was deserted, as Herodotos describes; and we find that the series of painted Greek vases left there came abruptly to an end. Then, the frontier being thus stripped and bare, the Babylonian came in. Nebuchadrezzar has left inscriptions of his in the isthmus of Suez, and he fought with Aahmes. Thus he doubtless occupied the fortress of Tahpanhes, and would naturally have his royal pavilion pitched upon the wide brick pavement in the cool shadow of the high fort.

46. *The Jews of Syene.*

We now turn to the opposite end of Egypt, for Jews were at both ends, and probably scattered over all the land between. Within the last few years many papyri have been brought to light at Aswan and the island of Elephantine, just below the first cataract. These show that Aramaic—the common language of Syria—was regularly used there, and we can readily see how "five cities in the land of Egypt speak the language of Canaan and swear to Yahveh of hosts" (Isa. xix, 19), as the oath in these papyri is by Yahu.

An insight into the considerable Jewish colony at Aswan—Syene—is given by the series of documents of one family, extending over sixty-one years, from 471–410 B.C. Other papyri report the destruction of the temple of Yahu in 410 B.C., the petition for its rebuilding 407 B.C., and the granting of the petition. The temple of Yahu, or Yahveh, is called simply the "altar of Yahu" in the family documents. It was of fair size, as it filled the space between two roads, and it had three private properties opposite to it, those of Zechariah, Yezanieh, and Hosea. There are altogether eleven plots of land and houses which are named to the south and west of the temple. The central figure of the documents is a woman, Mibhtahyah, daughter of Mahseiah. She was married to Yezanieh, son of Uriah, in 459 B.C., and in 440 B.C. to an Egyptian, As-hor, who took the name of Nathan. As-hor was dead by 421, but left, by her, two sons, Yedoniah and Mahseiah, who by 410 B.C. each appropriated one of the family slaves.

The condition socially seems to have been one of comfort, though not of wealth. The dowry of Mibhtahyah on her second marriage was 12 shekels for her outfit, and clothes to the value of 65 shekels; three large wrap-garments cost from 6 to 28 shekels each, a mirror, a bronze tray, and two bronze cups cost 1½ shekels each. The property was all to go to the survivor. Divorce was free without any penalty, on either party declaring it, standing up in the congregation; only the husband in either case got back all he had given. But there is a penalty of 200 shekels if the husband acknowledge any other wife or children; polygamy, therefore, was thought much worse than divorce. Witnesses were four to a minor deed, eight to a deed of lands, and twelve to important marriage settlements. Land was valuable in the town of Syene, an ordinary plot for a house being only 22 × 19 feet. The cost is not stated. Interest for money was at five per cent. per month.

The names were those which are familiar in the later time of the kingdom, such as Zechariah, Hananiah, Nathan, Shallum, and Menaham; the principal figure, Mibhtahyah, was named "Trust Yahveh," or "My confidence is in Yahveh." The community had their own law, administered in the court of the Hebrews. They swore in their deeds by Yahu; yet we also find a Jewish oath by Sati, goddess of the cataract. They were evidently accustomed to litigation, as every deed contains a clause against it; for instance: "I shall have no power, I and my children, and my descendants, and any one else, to institute against thee suit or process on account of this house. . . Moreover, no one else shall be able to produce against thee a deed whether new or old, except this deed which I have written and given thee. Whoever shall produce against thee a deed, I have not written it."

A violent blow to this peaceful community was the destruction of their temple of Yahu in 410. In the absence of the satrap Arsam, the priests of Khnum stirred up the local governor, Widrang, and got an order to destroy the Jewish temple, which the

Jews stated that even Cambyses had respected, when he attacked the Egyptian temples. This shows that before 525 B.C. the Jews already had their temple, with an altar, and sacrificial bowls of gold and silver. The temple was built of cut stones, with columns of stone, seven gates, and a roof of cedar. In 407 the community petitioned for the permission to rebuild this temple, and they were allowed to do so. Fortunately their petition, and the answer on papyrus, have been preserved, and show this remarkable position of the Egyptian Jews.

47. *The Earlier Type of Judaism.*

Thus within two generations of Nebuchadrezzar the Jewish quarter of Aswan was well established, owning and dealing with property. Later on, the second temple at Jerusalem was being built as the centre of Jewish worship, while there was this altar and temple of Yahveh of considerable size in the southern frontier of Egypt. And although the mention of a heathen god was an abomination to the returned exile, the woman named "Trust Yahveh" had no objection to swear by the goddess Sati, when dealing with an Egyptian. In short, the standpoint is that of the Jewish monarchy, and knows nothing of the particularity of the zealots, who left Babylon for the ideal of a Puritan life in Jerusalem, and who stamped their tone on subsequent Judaism. If this were the type of Egyptian Jew we can realise much more the rise of the Alexandrian Jewish literature, and the training of the eclectic Philo who worked for the union of Jewish thought with Greek philosophy.

CHAPTER VII

ISRAEL TRIUMPHANT IN EGYPT

THOUGH every school-child is supposed to know about the Jewish kings, however ephemeral, yet scarcely any one knows the striking features of Jewish history after the kingdom. Yet the violent persecutions, the two generations of an independent theocracy between the Greek and Roman conquests, and the great new centre of Judaism in Egypt, are as considerable and as picturesque events as most of those that we are familiar with in the earlier history. The importance of the Jewish sub-kingdom on the east of Egypt is shown by a side-light. We read that the land called after the High Priest Oniah, stretched from near Cairo down to the coast, and that the Jews who occupied it could bar the way of the auxiliaries of Caesar when passing from Syria to Alexandria.

48. *The Trouble in Judaea.*

The convulsion which left the deepest mark on Jewish thought between the two destructions of Jerusalem, was the attempt to force the Hellenization of the Jews, by Antiochos Epiphanes. Even the family of the High Priests joined the Gentile party. In 175 B.C. Jeshua, the brother of Oniah, bribed for the High Priesthood, with 360 talents of silver down, and 80 talents' tribute, and an offer of 150 talents more to set up a gymnasium with Jewish ephebi. The Temple was despised, the sacrifices neglected, and the priests went to play quoits. Offerings were sent by Jeshua to the quinquennial games of Herakles at Tyre, which even the messengers could not bring themselves to offer. Jeshua, however, was betrayed by his own deputy Menelaos, who took the tribute to Antiochos, and who outbid him by 300 talents. Menelaos, being then in power, stole the golden vessels of the deserted temple, partly for bribes, partly to sell. He then slew Oniah, who had been the rightful High Priest before Jeshua. A fierce civil war broke out between Jeshua and Menelaos; Antiochos came down to crush it, and, after a huge slaughter in Jerusalem, seized the pillage of the place, from which he carried out 1800 talents.

The temple was now dedicated to Zeus Olympios, and the Jews decked with ivy performed the Dionysiac festival. Unclean meats were to be eaten, and keeping the Sabbath and circumcision were punished with death.

49. *The Youth Oniah.*

Amid all these troubles, 169–166 B.C., there was growing up a boy, Oniah IV, whose father had been the High Priest, but had been murdered just before the evil days. The boy's uncles, Jeshua and Menelaos, had fought for the priesthood, and the successful competitor died about 160 B.C. The high priesthood was then taken from the old family, and given to an upstart; and the youth Oniah, dreading for his own safety, fled down into Egypt. Though Antiochos had died in 164 B.C., yet his policy was continued. The Hellenizing party, who were ready to accommodate Judaism to the state of the world around it, were openly at war with the puritans under Judas Maccabaeus. It was the ever-recurring tale of Pharisee and Sadducee, the Montanists and the Lapsed, the Fifth-monarchy men and Cromwell, the Non-jurors and William III, or the Wee-Frees and United Frees in Scotland to-day—the most difficult line of all to distinguish, between faithfulness and fanaticism, between common sense and cowardice. The fanatical Judas Maccabaeus may be otherwise looked on as the saviour-patriot, a second David, as he was held to be by the triumphant zealots afterwards. Beginning by a hard fight for religious toleration for himself, as soon as he had won that, he kept on fighting in order to destroy toleration for his opponents—a true covenanting puritan.

What course was possible for a man of the highest family, who had fled from the dire confusion as too perilous for life—who did not wish to be either faithless or fanatical? He saw around him myriads of his own kin, far from their Holy City and its observances, barred by politics and disturbances from even visiting it. Naturally they were sinking into more and more separation from their national life and religion. The young Oniah had served his new rulers, Ptolemy Philometor and Cleopatra, actively for several years, being the general of Cleopatra; and, rising in power and respect, he approached the question of some unification for his Jewish kin, and a regulation of their worship, long since cut off from that of Jerusalem.

50. *The Petition of Oniah.*

The official petition which he addressed to the king and the royal reply, are to be found in Josephus; but an opinion lately has been against the genuineness of these documents. In the petition Oniah states that the variety of Egyptian worships caused the Egyptians to have ill will against one another. This was a very natural thing for a Jew to say to a Greek king, who only officially recognised the Egyptian gods; and it was a skilful plea for starting a central temple for at least one large body of subjects, when the great danger to the Egyptian throne lay in disunion. Oniah then asked for a ruined Egyptian town sacred to Bubastis of the fields, which was deserted, and in which he wished to build a temple "after the pattern of that in Jerusalem and of the same dimensions," to ensure mutual harmony and submission to the king. He relied on the passage where Isaiah had prophesied about an altar being set up in the midst of Egypt, as a guiding reason for his course. The reply of Ptolemy grants his petition; but, with the fine sarcasm of a Gallio or a Gibbon, he wonders how the scrupulous and anti-idolatrous Jews get over the dedicating to their god an unclean heathen site. We have seen something like it just lately in the Jewish authorities accepting large bequests from a usurer as not inconsistent with denouncing usury. To set aside these letters as improbable because the Greek king had no objection to a reflection on Egyptian diversities, and was a little sarcastic about Jewish acquisitiveness, is to judge all historical material by the tone of a modern shopkeeper. If we do this, the "circle of Popilius," or Edward's message "to let the boy win his spurs" at Crecy, will have to be dropped because Brown, Jones, or Robinson would not have thought of doing business in that way. Half of history seems incredible to one who looks at all things through modern spectacles.

The petition being granted, Oniah did not succeed in doing all that he had named in his request, and unfulfilled concessions are not unknown in our own days. But he "built a temple and an altar to God, like indeed to that in Jerusalem, but smaller and poorer." It was also unlike Jerusalem because it was like a tower, built of large stones to 60 cubits high. This is to be expected if it were on an artificial mound, which had to be supported by a high revetment wall, instead of being on a natural rock as at Jerusalem. But all the description of the appearance and arrangements must be accepted, as we have them from a Jew who was contemporary with this temple, and very probably had actually seen it. So far our recorded information takes us; but for long past there has been the open question where this building was, and if any remains of it could yet be found.

51. *Discovery of the Temple of Oniah.*

In recent excavations at Tell el Yehudiyeh, about twenty miles north of Cairo, a high mound of sand attracted attention by its size, and by having been all thrown up at one time in the second century B.C., as shown by the pottery at the base and the top of it. This place is within the Heliopolite nome, and closely about 180 Egyptian stadia from Memphis, as the town of Oniah is described by Josephus. Also that town is stated to have been known before as Leontopolis, where the lion-headed goddess was worshipped; and, similarly, in this place was found a stone shrine of the lion-headed goddess, in the ruins of the Egyptian quarter. Every external condition was thus in accord; but what could be made out of the mound? The first thing to do was very tenderly to clear the loose rubbish from the top of it, and see if any trace of construction was left, after all the wrecking which has continued down to our own day. The bare sand-hill had only a few inches, or a foot or two, of dust and chips upon it, and to recover any forms of buildings seemed quite hopeless. Working over from the eastern side of the hill, first blocks of brickwork were met with, sunk in the ground, which had formed the foundations of a massive fortification wall along the edge of the platform. Next, a few bricks and a scrap of wall in line showed the foundation of an inner wall, and further on stood the base of the opposite wall of a court. Then, at the north end was a thick foundation, part of the outer wall, and across the court was another narrow foundation dividing it in two, forming an outer and inner court. At the south end of this was a very massive pile of brick foundation, 55 feet long and 17 feet wide, all of solid brickwork, excepting a narrow groove up the axis. Now, this is in the position where the temple itself should have been, and after allowing for a slight footing or ledge of brick foundation outside of the wall, we find that the building upon this would be of exactly the proportions of the temple. The actual size was 70 × 20 spans, instead of 70 × 20 cubits, as in Solomon's temple. What the size of Zerubbabel's temple was we have no record; but Herod, in his speech to the Jews, when he sought to remove it and build his grander temple, stated that Zerubbabel could not build so large a temple as Solomon, because he had to follow the measures fixed by Cyrus and Darius. It may well have been that, in the poverty of the return to Jerusalem from exile, the Jews could not attempt more than a reduced copy of the work of Solomon, a span for each cubit of the older dimension. The mass of foundation of this temple of Oniah had been many feet deeper than the portion which remained, so no trace could be found of the cross-walls of the porch and oracle, which are entered upon the plan from their place in Solomon's temple (Figs. 47, 48).

52. *The Courts and Approaches.*

On the north of the temple courts were two ascents; one, a great stairway from the plain below, hereafter described; the other, a slope up from the town, over ten feet wide. This approach was completely commanded by a building to the west, which rose up sheer over the ascent. The south side of the same building is also shown by foundations, and the north side is marked by a vertical face of the sand mound about ten feet high, showing where a wall has been removed. The large square building thus marked out, over 70 feet by 50 feet, is on the highest part of the mound (see model), and completely dominated the temple courts, the west face of the great mound, the northern town, and both of the approaches; it must have been the castle or citadel.

Of the great stairway from the plain there remain two thick walls of brick, still eleven feet high, although the upper part and all the stairs have been destroyed. This high raised ascent was fourteen feet wide, and is best realised from the model. The walls were nearly four feet thick, and between them the space is filled with over six feet of gravel and sand, to form a basis for the steps. The lower end of the ascent outside of the fortification was probably of timber, as there is only a large pier of brickwork built against the outer face of the town, and the whole of that part has been burnt through by a great conflagration. A wooden stairway here would be easily removed in case of warfare, so as to cut off the approach to the town.

53. *The Outer Wall.*

The outer defences of the whole town and temple have almost disappeared. On the east side is the only part showing the massive stone walling, where a portion was discovered still six courses high. This grand mass of wall was built of blocks nearly two

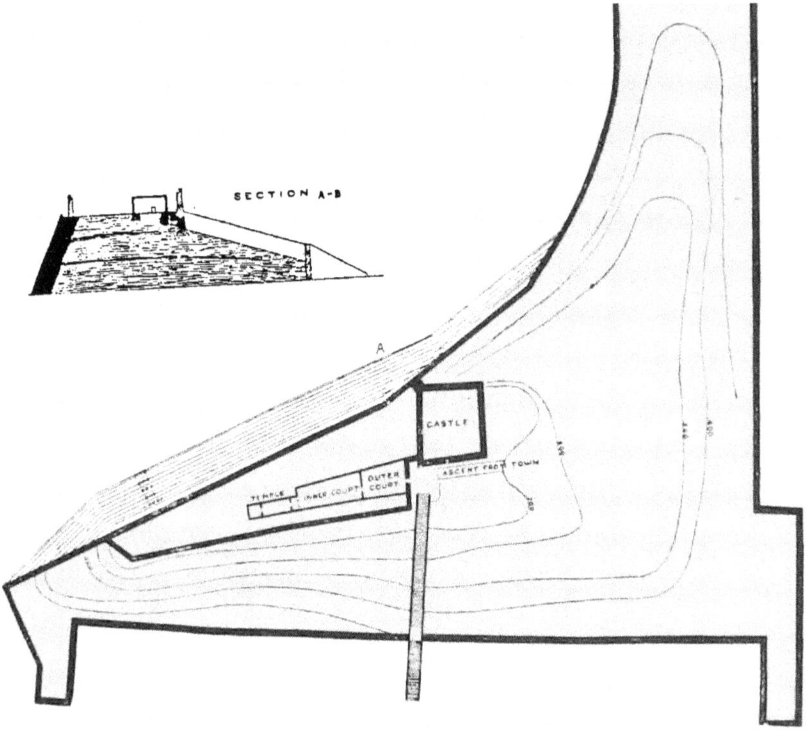

FIG. 47.—Plan of the city of Oniah, and the enclosure of the temple.

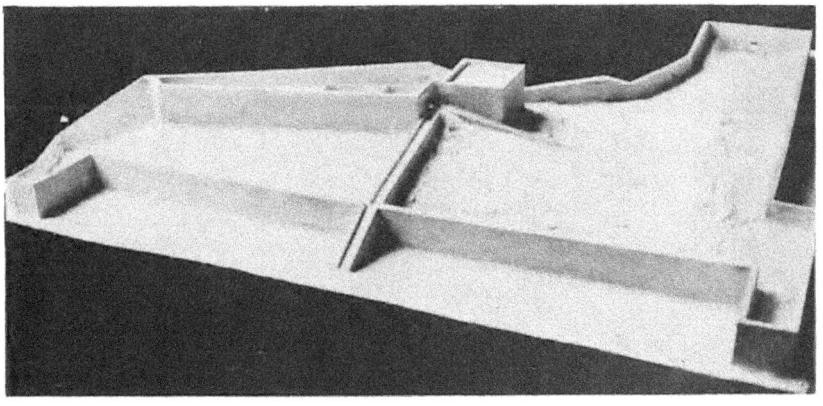

FIG. 48.—Model of the above, showing the relative heights of the parts.

To face page 104.

ashes about three inches thick, and the oven has been heated until the earth around it is reddened. Upon the ashes lie one or two leg-bones of a lamb. Now all this is exactly in accord with the passover ritual. The Mishna describes the pottery ovens as being like beehives, but open at the top to lower the lamb for roasting; and only leg-bones were to be cast into the fire, not any other parts. The uniform stratum of ashes shows that these ovens had been used to an equal amount, and that they had not been heated repeatedly for common cooking. The special use of them is shown by their only occurring at the old ground level, and not also high up in the mound. If they had been intended for workmen's fires they would not have been placed exactly where they would be buried at once in piling up the mound. The ovens were mostly sunk in the ground, but in other cases they stood on the surface, and were built round with brickwork and smoothly plastered.

Thus at the foundation of this new Jerusalem, Oniah summoned an immense assembly of the heads of Jewish families in Egypt. On the site of the new town the ovens for the passover were ranked in rows. As the sun went down the fires blazed from hundreds or thousands of ovens; the lambs were slain immediately after sunset, and soon they were roasting in the ovens for the solemn feast. When that was over all the assembled community threw in earth on the fires, and smothered them; thus they began to found the new city in the dying flames of sacrifice. There was a deep meaning in this, though not strictly orthodox. The Canaanites had sacrificed a child to place beneath their buildings: in the Jewish age it

FIG. 49.—Massive stone wall of the eastern enclosure of the city of Oniah.

is found in Palestine that a lighted lamp was covered with a bowl, and then built over with the foundations, thus killing a flame of fire instead of a life. Here this fire-killing was done on the largest scale, and the whole mound rests upon the extinguished fires of the sacrifices.

55. *The Jewish Remains.*

Though the mound has been ransacked for every scrap of stone, and all the brick walls carried away to throw on the fields, yet a few remains rewarded our clearance. One precious scrap of the accounts for delivery of bricks to the builders shows that Jews named Abram and Shabtai were thus employed. On the top of the mound a piece of the moulding of the temple was found, and a ram's horn from a sacrifice. About a generation ago, there was a vast pile of burnt bones of calves and lambs lying outside the city wall on the north, apparently the remains of the daily sacrifice. A few architectural fragments show that the architecture was Corinthian, but with Syrian features in the rounded battlements which crowned the walls. Half of a large column of grey marble was probably part of one of the two columns in the porch of the temple. This and other fragments are now all preserved at University College, London.

Beside all the evidence that has now been found there should be noted the cemetery with Jewish gravestones found by Dr. Naville twenty years ago on the desert, to which a road leads from this city. And the name of this place, "Mound of the Jewess," also agrees with the connection that we have now described.

56. *Authority of Josephus.*

One lesson from these discoveries is that we should respect our ancient authorities more, and not treat them as the sport of every writer who wishes to parade his cleverness at negation. Josephus has been accused of discrepancies because he states that Oniah asked leave to build a temple like that at Jerusalem, but he actually built it smaller and poorer and like a tower. The difficulties of so large an enterprise, and the need of a vast revetment wall to hold up the mound where they wished it to be steep, caused both these differences, and the actual facts reconcile the statements of the text. Josephus states that the temple rose to 60 cubits from the ground below, and the actual remains found guarantee a height of at least 59 cubits. Many writers have confused Heliopolis city with the nome, Josephus is always correct in placing the city of Oniah in the Heliopolite nome or county, but at the correct distance from Memphis. The more facts we can ascertain, the less are we inclined to cry out on errors and discrepancies in our authorities.

57. *The New Jerusalem in Egypt.*

When we can now get a whole view of the city of Oniah it is seen how it was as close a copy as could be arranged of the Temple hill at Jerusalem. The whole of this artificial mound of about six acres, and seventy feet high to the platform, was set at the north-east corner of the older Egyptian town just as the temple stood on the north-east of the older town of Jerusalem. Between the town wall and the great revetment wall of this mound there was a narrow gap, running up to a passage three times as deep as it was wide. This was in imitation of the steep gorge of the Tyropoion valley at Jerusalem, which was bridged over, but which is now filled with rubbish. On the east side this mound sloped down at the same angle as the fall into the Kedron valley. The tapering end of this mound to the south must have been much like what the Temple hill was before Herod built out his great platform on substructures, now known as Solomon's stables. The great stairway here is exactly in the position of the great ceremonial stairway up which the processions went singing "songs of degrees." When I was at Jerusalem in 1891 I found the lower steps of a wide stairway cut in the rock, opposite the north end of the Haram area; and evidently the slope from those steps must have run up on a high crest of masonry raised some distance above the hill-side slope. So here the stairway was raised in this manner. Here the castle is exactly in the place of the Castle of Antonia, which was certainly as old as the Maccabees; in both cases the castles join the north-west corner of the temple courts, and command the courts, northern town, and the old town on the west. And here a new town was built to the north of the castle and temple in the walled enclosure; so at Jerusalem, the Bezetha or new quarter lay in the same position. Thus the whole was planned to be as close an imitation of the topography of the temple hill as could be arranged on a small scale. To do this, and yet form so defensible a stronghold, with such excellent protective arrangements, was indeed a skilful piece of design.

The wreck of the whole came after Titus had taken Jerusalem, and when the Zealots tried in utter folly to start a revolt in the Jewish region of the Eastern Delta. This mad attempt could not be tolerated in the valuable province of Egypt: so the temple was closed, after its treasures had been removed. Thus the place fell into decay and perished, being stripped in our own days of all the stonework and brick, until it seemed a shapeless sand-hill. Little by little the last traces of the structures have now been discovered, and we can just recover the outlines of this centre of Judaism before it passes into hopeless oblivion, and the place thereof shall know it no more.

CHAPTER VIII

THE FORERUNNERS OF CHRISTIANITY

58. *The Growth of Thought.*

THE general ignorance regarding the development of religious thought around the Eastern Mediterranean during the centuries before our era, has given a very false impression regarding the ideas and terms of speech found in the New Testament. Because to most readers religious literature is a blank from Malachi to Matthew, there is a general sense of there having been stagnation during four centuries. Yet those centuries were an age of excessive mixture and ferment of new ideas. The previous four centuries from Joel to Malachi were tranquil in comparison; the succeeding four centuries, from John the Baptist to Cyril, were hardly more revolutionary than the age of interaction of Jew and Greek, Median and Persian, Egyptian and Phrygian, which preceded Christianity.

If we are to understand the literature of any age, we must know the general thoughts and phraseology of the time, which are used in it. Could we expect a foreigner to understand Johnson who had only read Chaucer previously? Who would see the position of John Wesley if he only knew Piers Plowman or

Thomas à Kempis? The current thought and expression is the essential basis for beginning to understand the nature, the sense, the appeal, of any new religious movement.

And the fundamental body of Christian literature is no exception to this general principle. If we are to see what the meaning of it was to those to whom it was addressed and who used it, we must first realise how they thought, what terms they used, what basis was built upon, and so learn to distinguish what were the new ideas and new terms then brought forward.

59. *The Hermetic Books.*

This position has been considerably explained to us recently by finding the dating of the so-called Hermetic books, which by their historical allusions are now seen to belong to the age between Zerubbabel and Antiochos the Great, 500–200 B.C. As the whole matter rests on this dating, we will here give an outline of it.

In the *Korē Kosmou*, or Virgin Creation of the World, is a comparison to a good satrap, which stamps it to the Persian good government of Egypt, before 400 B.C.; and it is said that the satrap bestows the fruits of his victory upon the vanquished, a peculiar reference to a unique event, when, after the Persians vanquished Egypt, they led the Egyptians on westward to the plunder of Cyrene. The references to Egyptian terms and ideas agree also to this date. In the Definitions of Asklepios, or Imhotep, hatred of Greek translation is expressed, and the king is called Ammon; now, the last Egyptian king descended in theory from the god Amon was Nectanebo, 359–342 B.C., and after his date Greek became the fashionable official language. In the Perfect Sermon is a well-known passage on the destruction of Egyptian temples and worship, and the massacre of the people by Scythian and Indian. This can only refer to the second Persian invasion, 342–332 B.C., when such events took place, and Scythian and Indian were the western and eastern branches of the Persian army; the Egyptian allusions agree also with this date. In the treatise on the Universal Mind, the civilised world is referred to as Egypt and Persia and Greece, again showing the prominence of the Persian empire, as it was before Alexander. With such definite allusions as these, and the absence of a single allusion to later times or peoples, we must accept the age of these religious works as above stated, and see in them the development of religious thought in Egypt under Persian and Indian influence, which formed a basis of later Jewish and Greek developments.

60. *Beliefs on the Godhead.*

The most important of the growths of belief that we can trace is that in the division of the Godhead. At 500 B.C. the belief was in a supreme Creator God, with many subordinate gods and guardian angels. The next stage, by 350 B.C., represented God as the Universal Maker, all are parts of God, and God is All, for the fullness or completion of all things is One. At 340 B.C. God is described as All in One and One in All. But a difficulty arose—which is explained later by Philo—that as an imperfect and changing world could not emanate from an unchanging God, therefore some intermediary must be supposed. Hence a Second God, who could be regarded as not eternal and immutable, was required as an intermediary. So the conclusion was that the Lord and Maker of All from Himself made the Second God, the Visible and Perceptible, whom He loved as His Son. And as man, being finite, could not comprehend the infinite, so man was made to contemplate the Son. Before 332 B.C. we find named the good Spirit, Agatho-Daimon, who is the First-born God.

61. *The Logos.*

In the earlier time there is no mention of reason or Logos, but by 350 B.C. the Logos is described as the rational part of the soul, and is said to be above the daimons. Before 332 B.C. the human Reason or Logos is reverenced, as in the saying, "Unto this Logos, son, thy adoration and thy worship pay."

This developed further in the statements that "With Logos (reason), not with hands did the Creator make the universal Kosmos." Yet it was a general faculty, not personified, as "Man did excel by reason of the Logos," and "Logos indeed among all men He hath distributed."

Next this divine reason begins to be personified. "Thy Logos sings through me Thy praises," and "Send thou oblation acceptable to God, but add, my son, too, 'through the Logos.'"

When we reach the last and most developed of the Hermetic books, "The Shepherd of Men," we read, "A Holy Logos descended on that Nature," and "Earth and water no one could discern, yet were they moved to hear by reason of the Logos pervading them," and "The Logos that appeared from Mind is Son of God," and "Holy art Thou who didst by Logos make to consist the things that are."

Here we see the gradual growth in the logical necessity of a second Divine nature in contact with the world, the gradual rise of the view of reason as a personification, and the union of the ideas in the personified reason or Logos being the Second God.

When we reach the latest pre-Christian stage, in the writings of Philo, the whole dogma is rounded and complete. "It was not possible that anything subject to death could be imaged after the supremest God, who is the Father of the universes, but rather after the Second God who is His Logos." "The Logos is God's likeness by whom the whole Kosmos was fashioned." "The Logos is called Dominion, and Name of God, and Reason, and Man-after-his-likeness, and Seeing Israel." "God, as Shepherd and King, leads with law and justice the nature of the heavens, deputing His own Logos, His first-born Son, to take charge of the sacred flock, as though he were the Great King's viceroy, His eldest Son, whom elsewhere He hath called His First-born, and who fashions the species." "The Man of God who, being the Logos of the Eternal, is of necessity Himself eternal."

From the close connection between the Hermetic writings and all that we know of the tenets of the

Essenes and Therapeutae, the ascetics of Judaea and Egypt, it seems that this development of theology belonged to the Essenes. Hence, we can easily understand how a pious man, whose youth had been spent with the Essenes, and who had been impressed with this theology, would see its applicability to the development of Christianity, and lay his foundations in the doctrine that the Logos was with God, and the Logos was God, and all things were made by him. And how, in view of the doctrine that the Logos of the Eternal is of necessity himself eternal, he would say that the Logos was, in the beginning, with God. The opening of the Gospel of St. John is the Essene view of the new doctrine of the Way.

62. *Types of Conversion.*

Another belief which grew up during this period is that of an abiding change in the individual mind, a definite conversion. There was no such idea in the older Egyptian religion, nor do we find it in the *Korē Kosmou* (500 B.C.). But by 350 B.C. it is said that if a ray of God shines through the sun into the soul, the daimons do not act upon the soul, while all other men are led and driven by the daimons. As this work is particularly anti-Greek, the idea seems to be Oriental, either Egyptian or imported from India or Persia.

In the Perfect Sermon (340 B.C.) it is said that some men have won such rapture that they have obtained a share of Divine sense. A little later is the treatise on the Font of Mind, in which a man is to be immersed that he might become a partaker in the Gnosis or Divine knowledge. Probably some form of baptism, as a ceremony, preceded this dogmatic use of the emblem; but it shows what was the primitive sense of baptism, and is reflected later by the baptism of John, being immediately followed by the descent of the Spirit on the baptized.

In the Secret Sermon another simile is used, that of re-birth : "Whenever I see within myself the sincere vision brought to birth out of God's mercy, I have passed through myself into a body that can never die. And now I am not what I was before, but I am born in Mind." "Who is the author of Re-birth? The Son of God, the one Man, by God's will." "The natural body which our sense perceives is far removed from this essential birth. The first must be dissolved, the last can never be dissolved. The first must die, the last death cannot touch. Dost thou not know thou hast been born a God, son of the One?" No man can be saved before re-birth; he must first become a stranger to the illusion of the world. Those re-born in mind have passed through self into an undying body. To reach re-birth, throw out of work the bodily senses, and withdraw into thyself; will it, and the divinity shall come to birth. The doctrine of re-birth is to be kept secret or esoteric. In all this there is a strong Indian influence; the re-birth, and the trance state of introspection through which it is attained, are both from the early Indian theosophy.

63. *Links with Christianity.*

Here we see how the accepted religious metaphors and terms were used later in "the true Light, which coming into the world lighteth every man," in the baptism to confer the Divine Spirit, in the teaching "that which is born of the flesh is flesh, and that which is born of the Spirit is spirit. . . . Except a man be born again he cannot see the kingdom of God." It is notable how two of these three similes only occur in the Gospel of John, which also shows the adaptation of the Logos doctrine.

There are also, beside these great dogmas, separate examples of thought, which show the current ideas that were continued later into the New Testament. We read that in part man is deathless, in part subject to death while in the body, much as Paul writes, "Who shall deliver me from this body of death?" Again, all are parts of God, and God is All, "for all things are from Him, in Him, and through Him," as Paul writes, "Of Him, and through Him, and unto Him are all things." Again, it is said that either flood or fire or pestilence shall purify the world, and all good things shall be made new, as Peter anticipates that the world, having in the past been purified by flood, the heavens and earth that now are, are reserved unto fire, preparatory to a new heavens and new earth, wherein dwell righteousness.

We see thus how much the development of religious thought and expression had grown, before it was adopted by Christianity as the current phraseology of pious minds, and as natural forms of expression for the teaching of further religious beliefs.

64. *Pauline Use of the Book of Wisdom.*

Not only can we gather the religious language of these earlier centuries from the Hermetic books, but the later two centuries, from 200 B.C., are well illustrated by the Apocrypha. In particular, the Book of Wisdom was specially familiar to Paul, and its terms and phrases and lines of thought were constantly in his mind. In the Book of Ecclesiastes there is no trace of the personification of wisdom ; in that of Ecclesiasticus, written about 180 B.C., Wisdom is fully personified. So about 200 B.C. is the age of the rise of Wisdom literature, which succeeded the Hermetic books, and which does not appear in those earlier works. The Book of the Wisdom of Solomon is to be dated between 200 and 100 B.C.

For the sake of here comparing the passages, those from the Book of Wisdom are put in the first column, those from the New Testament in the second column.

Of Wisdom—Sophia—herself, we read—

Wisdom is a loving spirit (i, 6).	The fruit of the Spirit is love (Gal. v, 22).
Love is the keeping of her laws (vi, 18).	Love is the fulfilling of the law (Rom. xiii, 10).
Wisdom is an understanding spirit . . . undefiled, not subject to hurt, loving the thing which is good . . . kind to man, stedfast, sure, free from care, overseeing all things, and going through all understanding (vii, 22, 23).	Charity suffereth long and is kind . . . seeketh not her own . . . thinketh no evil . . . endureth all things (1 Cor. xiii, 4-7).
Wisdom . . . is the brightness of the everlasting light, the unspotted mirror of the power of God, and the image of His goodness (vii, 26).	The brightness of His glory and the express image of His person (Heb. i, 3).

Wisdom shall not ... dwell in the body that is subject unto sin (i, 4).	I am carnal, sold under sin (Rom. vii, 14). Know ye not that your body is the temple of the Holy Ghost? (1 Cor. vi, 19).

Of the wise it is said—

They shall judge the nations (iii, 8).	The saints shall judge the world (1 Cor. vi, 2).
Grace and mercy is to His saints (iii, 9).	Grace, mercy, and peace (1 Tim. i, 2).
They shall receive ... a beautiful crown from the Lord's hand (v, 16).	There is laid up for me a crown of righteousness which the Lord ... shall give me (2 Tim. iv, 8).
He shall put on righteousness as a breastplate, and true judgment as a helmet. He shall take holiness for an invincible shield. His severe wrath shall he sharpen for a sword (v, 18–20).	Having on the breastplate of righteousness ... taking the shield of faith ... and take the helmet of salvation and the sword of the Spirit (Ephes. vi, 14–17).

Of the heathen, a natural religion is recognised—

Vain are all men by nature who are ignorant of God, and could not out of the good things that are seen know him that is ... but deemed ... the lights of heaven to be the gods which governed (xiii, 1, 2).	That which may be known of God is manifest ... so they are without excuse ... and changed the glory of the incorruptible God into an image (Rom. i, 19–23).
For by the greatness and beauty of the creatures, proportionably the maker of them is seen (xiii, 5).	The invisible things ... are clearly seen, being understood by the things that are made (Rom. i, 20).
They peradventure err, seeking God and desirous to find Him (xiii, 6).	They should seek the Lord, if haply they might feel after Him and find Him (Paul in Acts xvii, 27).

THE FORERUNNERS OF CHRISTIANITY

So there reigned in all men blood, manslaughter, etc., etc. (xiv, 25).

God gave them over to a reprobate mind, etc., etc. (Rom. i, 28).

Thou canst do all things, and winkest at the sins of men because they should amend (xi, 23).

The times of this ignorance God winked at (Paul in Acts xvii, 30).

If Thou didst punish the enemies ... with such deliberation ... with how great circumspection wilt Thou judge Thine own sons? (xii, 20, 21).

God ... endured with long-suffering the vessels of wrath ... that He might make known the riches of His glory on the vessels of mercy (Rom. ix, 22, 23).

Who shall say, What hast Thou done? (xii, 12).

Shall the thing formed say to him that formed it, Why hast thou made me? (Rom. ix, 20).

The potter of the same clay he maketh both the vessels that serve for clean uses, and likewise also all such as serve to the contrary (xv, 7).

Hath not the potter power over the clay, of the same lump to make one vessel unto honour and another unto dishonour? (Rom. ix, 21).

What man is he that can know the counsel of God? or who can think what the will of the Lord is? (ix, 13).

Who hath known the mind of the Lord? or who hath been His counsellor? (Rom. xi, 34).

There are also many general statements, such as—

O ye kings, ... power is given you of the Lord (vi, 1–3).

The powers that be are ordained of God (Rom. xiii, 1).

He which is Lord over all shall fear no man's person (vi, 7).

For there is no respect of persons with God (Rom. ii, 11; Gal. ii, 6; Ephes. vi, 9; Col. iii, 25).

All men have one entrance into life, and the like going out (vii, 6).

We brought nothing into this world, and certain we can carry nothing out (1 Tim. vi, 7).

For the corruptible body presseth down the soul, and the earthly tabernacle weigheth down the mind (ix, 15).	For we that are in this tabernacle do groan being burdened (2 Cor. v, 4).
For there is no word so secret that shall go for nought (i, 11).	Every idle word that men shall speak they shall give account thereof (Matt. xii, 36).
Beware of murmuring (i, 11).	Do all things without murmurings (Phil. ii, 14).
He pleased God and was beloved of him, so that living among sinners he was translated (iv, 10).	Enoch was translated . . . for . . . he pleased God (Heb. xi, 5).

These resemblances, it will be seen, are never quotations, or references to narratives, but are a part of the common stock of ideas and expressions of the later writer; and they underlie not only these direct identities, but also are seen in whole passages. Thus the whole chapter x. is the basis of construction in Heb. xi; and chapters xii, 24 to end of xiv are parallel to Romans i. Evidently the Book of Wisdom was the familiar base of religious thought to Paul, and he naturally fell into parallelism of construction or of phrase, in his own writing. The passages quoted here are—

2 of Paul in Acts.
9 of Romans.
3 of 1 Corinthians.
1 of 2 Corinthians.
1 of Galatians.
1 of Ephesians.
1 of Philippians.
1 of Colossians.
2 of 1 Timothy.
1 of 2 Timothy.
2 of Hebrews.

Except, then, one reference to the importance of words, in Matthew, all the quotations belong to writings which have been attributed with more or less reason to Paul. The cause of this probably is that Wisdom was only in the Greek version, and therefore only a writer familiar with Greek in his youth would be saturated with it. This does not necessarily imply that Paul wrote all of the works in which these allusions occur, though the two passages in Paul's speeches in Acts strongly show the general correctness of the reporter. The authorship of the Hebrews and some other writings may be due to some other Greek-bred Jew. Apollos with a Greek name, born at Alexandria, and other Jews like him, may have been as familiar with the Book of Wisdom as we see Paul to have been.

We can now begin to see, from the Hermetic books and the Apocrypha, how much religious thought had moved in the centuries of the Dispersion, what a general basis there was for the implanting of the new ideas of Christianity, how easily the doctrine of the Logos and of Conversion served as vehicles for the Teaching of the new Way, and how continuous had been the movement of thought between the age of the Prophets and that of the Apostles.

CHAPTER IX

THE GROWTH OF THE GOSPELS

65. *The Light from the Logia.*

OF all discoveries in Egypt perhaps none has been of more general interest than that of two little tattered scraps of papyrus. These brought before us, for the first time, the actual examples of the collections of sayings, or "Logia of Jesus," which preceded the Gospels. Such Logia were mentioned by ancient writers, and their existence was recognised; but yet they were rather a literary abstraction, which was hardly realised. In these loose leaves from the dusty rubbish-mounds of Oxyrhynchus we at last saw before us the copies of the earliest Christian documents. Though the present leaves were a century or more later than the Gospel period, they were copied from far older writings. When once the Gospels were accepted and spread as standards of faith, there would be no room for starting collections of loose sayings, though various apocryphal narratives might arise. The stage of Logia, or disconnected sayings, is obviously that of personal memory of teaching, while the course of events was so fresh as not to

THE GROWTH OF THE GOSPELS 125

need formal narration. This preceded the form of a Gospel in which the sayings are connected by narratives and explanations of the circumstances.

It has been supposed too often that there were no early writings in the Church, but that during a generation or more everything rested on memory and oral teaching. This, however, would be contrary to what we now know about the use of writing commonly by the lower classes in Roman times. The papyri show that every 'trivial detail of life was written about freely, as at the present time; and the badness of the writing, as well as the positions of the writers—such as peasants and cooks—show that writing was a common art, and not restricted to educated people. Hence we should in any case expect that sayings and teaching would be recorded long before a full narration was required. Further, the disciples included at least one ready writer, for in three Gospels there is the account of the call of Matthew a tax-gatherer, who had always been writing receipts such as those we find commonly in Egypt. Thus it is clear how the Logia, or collections of sayings, were a natural first stage of Christian record, before more formal narratives were needed.

These documents from Egypt thus call our attention to the fact that the Gospels probably contained much material that was already on record; and that the labour of the evangelist was largely that of a compiler of documents already existing. The fact of compilation is clearly stated in the introduction to the Gospel according to St. Luke. How far, then, can we follow this clue, and discern the stages of compilation? How far can we distinguish the various materials used? These are the questions suggested by the papyri of the Logia.

Now, if we have three different arrangements of similar materials, such as in the three Synoptic Gospels, it is obvious that no two writers are likely to insert a saying or narrative independently at the same point, in a Gospel which is already in the hands of both. Still less is this likely to be done by three writers. Hence all materials which the different writers have used independently, is not to be expected to be put in similar order by each. And all that is stated by the three writers in identical order must be the basis or nucleus which was in the hands of all the writers to start with, and upon which they have each built their different Gospels.

66. *The Nucleus of the Gospels.*

This Nucleus is the earliest stage of the Gospels which we can thus prove, and it is about a quarter of the length of a whole Gospel. But it doubtless had also grown out of earlier material, and we can see some insertions in it which break the connection of the sense. It is therefore to be taken as the latest stage of united growth, before the separation of the Gospels; it is the trunk of the tree at the point where the branches begin to fork from it.

When we look at the material in the Nucleus we see some striking peculiarities. There is not any idea in it which outsteps the earliest form of teaching, that of fulfilling the law. There is no trace of the acceptance of the Gentiles. Further, even the Galilean history is very vaguely mentioned in it without a single place or person there being named. It seems to be entirely a Jerusalem document for the Early Church, while Galilee was still "of the Gentiles," and records of the Galilean ministry were disregarded.

The elimination of material which had been added to the Nucleus naturally brings together again long-sundered links. After the call of Simon and Andrew (Matt. iv, 22) the visit to Simon's house directly follows (viii, 14). After mentioning the bringing of the sick (viii, 16) a case of palsy is next described (ix, 2). The new doctrines are compared with the patch in the old garment, and the new wine (ix, 7), followed next by the eating corn and healing upon the Sabbath (xii, 1). The perplexity of Herod (xiv, 1) is followed by the answering paragraph (xvi, 13–16). The setting a child in the midst (xviii, 1–5) joins to children being brought to be blessed (xix, 13), though in Luke no less than nine chapters have been interpolated between the two halves of the episode.

Thus the Nucleus is by no means an arbitrary mechanical abstraction produced by taking only what is in identical order, but it has a very well-marked character as a document of the earliest period, and it is seen to be far more consecutive in its links than is the completed Gospel.

67. *How the Evangelists used the Documents.*

The next stage of growth that we can distinguish is that of two Gospels being in accord while a third differs in its order or contents. The peculiar fact appears that Mark agrees with Luke for the earlier third of his Gospel, while he agrees with Matthew for the other two-thirds. The only explanation of this seems to be that Mark and Luke wrote in common for a time, and after that Luke was not accessible, and therefore Mark copied Matthew so far as he had then added to the Nucleus. Mark thus preserves to us an early stage of the growth of the separate Gospels of Matthew and Luke before they had reached their present size. No theory of Mark being copied by Matthew and Luke can agree to these facts.

The third stage of growth is that of quoting from documents in different connections in the different Gospels. When we see how Luke has quoted from the Sermon on the Mount it appears that he read it through and inserted quotations from it exactly in the original order (Luke vi, 20 to x, 16). He then read it through again, and quoted nearly in order from it in chapters xi to xiii. Lastly, he read it a third time, quoting in chapter xvi. This curious use of a document, which we know of in a complete form, shows what we may expect.

We can thus recognise other documents which have been quoted from by two evangelists, but which are not given completely anywhere. We find one document from which fifteen passages have been quoted in identical order by Matthew and Luke, yet scattered over sixteen chapters of Matthew and nine chapters of Luke. The chances against fifteen scattered verses being in the same order in two writers, if they were not quoting from a single document, are too great to be worth considering. Obviously there was a common source for the order. And it had been thus extracted by Matthew and Luke before

Mark drew upon either of them for his Gospel. This was a Galilean document with an early form of commission to the disciples, before the list of apostles was thought needful. In like manner we can thus trace other documents similarly scattered, but in identical order of the fragments.

The latest materials added to the Gospels were the episodes which have no connection of position, or which are only found in a single writer.

We cannot here enter on the details of this inquiry, or the historical results seen on studying the stages of growth in relation to the development of the Church; these will be found in *The Growth of the Gospels*. But we have seen here how fruitful are the suggestions made by the scattered leaves of the *Logia*, which show the stage of record earlier than that of connected narrative.

CHAPTER X

EGYPT AND CHRISTIANITY

68. *The Jewish Position.*

IT might be thought that on reaching the Christian age we had parted from our subject of Egypt and Israel. Such was not the view of the first four centuries. Christianity began as the sect of Judaism which followed the Way; it was taught in the Temple as its home; it looked on Judaism as the necessary road to reach the new Way. Even when this, its first form, had been forcibly modified by the conditions of its growth, yet it was rooted in the Old Testament as its essential literature. This is strikingly seen as late as the fourth century, in the interesting Italian series of gold-in-glass designs. Among these there are seventeen subjects from the Jewish books and only six from the Gospels. And a similar prominence of Jewish subjects is found in the Catacomb paintings and the Mosaics. The importance of the Jewish outlook is seen as late as the fifth century, in the great mosaic of Santa Sabina, where stand the colossal figures of the "Church of the Jews," and the "Church of the Gentiles." Hence in the relations of Egypt to early Christianity we are

Fig. 50.—"The Church of the Circumcision," showing that as late as 430 A.D. the Jewish and Gentile Churches were regarded as on a par.

EGYPT AND CHRISTIANITY 131

still looking at the contact of Egypt and Israel (Figs. 50, 51).

69. *The Source of the Agapé.*

One of the most curious institutions of early Christianity was the Agapé, or love-feast, which it is hard for us to realise because all trace of it has so entirely died out. The careful study of the subject by Dr. Keating seems to show that the real character of it was a feast of brotherly love, in which occurred the Supper of Divine love, as part of one ceremony; that owing to persecution the two offices were separated in the second century; and that by the end of the fourth century the Agapae were almost extinct. The Council of Laodicea in 363 made it unlawful "to eat or set out couches in the house of God"; and the Council of Carthage in 397 forbade "banquets in a church." Yet such were still the custom in Rome in honour of Peter, as Paulinus writes of " crowds of the poor . . . gathered together into the magnificent basilica of the glorious Peter . . . all being fed with abundance of food."

Now, looking to the origin of this custom, it seems to have been accepted by the Apostles, but not instituted by them or enjoined. The source of it has been sought in Pagan feasts of religious fraternities, in the Essene feasts, in the Pharisees' feasts of brotherhood, and in the ceremonial routine of Jewish meals. None of these are so close to the Agapé as to have entirely originated it. But there is one marked feature which is apparently peculiar to Egypt, and which was in the very essence of the Agapé. It was held as a part of a religious service, and in the very building used for worship. Elsewhere this is apparently only true of the Therapeutae, out of all the proposed comparisons. They held a service every seven days, followed by anointing, and eating their allowed food together. While every seven weeks they held a feast together, followed by singing and religious dances. Evidently the service and the feast were both held conjoined in one place of assembly. Nor was this idea peculiar to the Egyptian Therapeutae, but it was a pagan custom in Egypt to feast in the temples. "Chairemon requests your company at dinner at the table of the lord Sarapis, in the Sarapaion to-morrow, the 15th, at the ninth hour,"—so runs a papyrus invitation of the second century.

It appears, then, that the love-feast of the Egyptian Therapeutae was adopted by the communistic early Church, becoming the surrounding ceremony of the more purely religious Supper. There was a similar survival in the North, where in the Heimskringla we read, "It was the olden custom that when a blood-offering should be, all the bonders should come into the place where was the Temple, bringing with them all the victuals they had need of while the feast should last; and at that feast should all men have ale with them." Yule was one of the main feasts of ale-drinking in the Norse Temple; and this was continued, as Christmas was the great season for Church Ales in England. In Cornwall the people each supplied food to the common feast. Here Christianity kept up the earlier connection of a feast along with the religious service in the place of worship.

The feasts at tombs were usual among the

Fig. 51.—"The Church of the Gentiles." In the church of Santa Sabina, Rome.

Egyptians; they were maintained till late times, as seen by the variety of food remains found in the Roman tomb-chapels at Hawara, and they are still kept up by Muhammedans. This custom likewise affected the Agapé, when it was held in honour of martyrs at their graves. Theodoret (429) writes of such yearly feasting; Augustine says, "I know many who drink most lavishly over the dead"; and the festival in honour of Peter we have quoted already. Here, again, an Egyptian custom seems to have been adopted by the Church.

70. *The Earliest Monasticism.*

Perhaps the greatest effect that Egypt had on the Church was at a time when the Agapé was disappearing, and a new type of brotherhood was eagerly adopted. Monasticism started as a system in Christianity with Pachomios, who founded the first community at Tabennisi in 322 A.D. But this first Christian monk had been a pagan monk of Sarapis, and for the roots of the system we must go to pre-Christian times. As early as 340 B.C. we find that there had sprung up an ascetic community in the desert behind the Fayum province. This was in opposition to all the thoughts and feelings of the Mediterranean world at that time. In Egypt, in Judaism, in Greece, we look in vain for any ascetic ideal. The only prototype for it is in the Buddhist monasticism, which was already organised, and was actively preached in the West by the date of 259 B.C. This was of the contemplative solitary type, like that of the early Egyptian recluses. That such influence of the Buddhist ideals should reach Egypt is what might be expected during the Persian hold on the Nile valley, 525 to 405 B.C. The presence of a large body of Indian troops in the Persian army in Greece 480 B.C., shows how far west the Indian connections were carried; and the discovery of modelled heads of Indians at Memphis, of about the fifth century B.C., shows that Indians were living there for trade. Hence there is no difficulty in regarding India as the source of the entirely new ideal of asceticism in the West.

After the mention of a community in the desert behind the Fayum about 340 B.C., we next hear of the recluses of the Sarapaion at Memphis about 170 B.C.; and the same class appears in 211 A.D. A development of this life was that of the Egyptian Therapeutae, who were mainly near Alexandria, and probably from them branched the Essenes of Judaea. It may be, however, that the Essene asceticism descends from the Buddhist mission to Antiochos, 259 B.C. That this Indian teaching—the "Law of Piety"—could be assimilated by Jews and Egyptians, is seen in the nature of it, that "all sects and creeds are in fundamental agreement about essentials" (Vincent Smith, *Asoka*, p. 25). There was no positive Theism to conflict with any other religion, but only a Law of Conduct which all religions might accept with advantage.

Thus Egypt was the channel by which monasticism was introduced into the Christian system. After the great step of the monk of Sarapis in 322, Rome took up the new ideal within a generation, and before the end of that century the Roman world was permeated with it.

71. What was before Time.

As in the realm of practice, Egypt had dominated Christianity by its monasticism, so also in the realm of dogma the greatest struggle was that between two Egyptians, which fatally involved the whole Empire, and led to the overthrow of that great Gothic dominion which might have steered the world clear of the barbarism of the Middle Ages. Such were the immense consequences of a dispute as to whether "before time" means "from eternity." Such a difference in the conception of a period before the existence of time would seem purely academic and indifferent to a Western mind. Constantine at first wrote that it was of little importance, and that the opposing parties should drop the subject, and not distract the Church.

To the Egyptian mind, however, this difference was in the essence of things. From early ages there had been two different words for what we call eternity. The root *heh* means anything vast and immeasurable; it is used of the inundation and of countless numbers; with the *ne* prefix it becomes *neheh*, literally "Belonging to vastness," or Eternity. A quite different idea is the eternity of duration of a king, for which *zet-ta* is used, literally "Creation of the world," that is, time belonging to physical things.

On coming to the later Egyptian works we find the same distinction. In the Korē Kosmou (500 B.C.) there is a long account of the creation of souls, and their rebellion, before the creation of the world. In the Perfect Sermon (340 B.C.) it is said that Eternity transcends the bounds of Time, but Time having no limits is of the nature of Eternity. Rather later (in

Corp. Herm. ix) Kosmos is the Second God after His image, that cannot die; and, though ever living, Kosmos is not eternal because it was created by the Eternal. Here before the idea of the Second God had been applied to a Personality, yet it was said not to be eternal because it proceeded from the Eternal. This is almost exactly the position of Arius in later times, as applied to the Christian conception of the Second God. Arius wrote, "God was not always a Father. He was God alone and solitary before He was the Father, and afterwards He became a Father. The Son had not always a being, for, as all other creatures were made out of nothing, so likewise was the Logos of God; and there was a time when He was not; nor had He any being till He was created. . . . God created a certain Person whom He called His Logos, His Wisdom, and His Son, that He might be His agent in the work of our creation" (Athanasius, 1st Oration). "Others, again, hold that the Logos Himself then became the Son when He was made man; for from being the Logos, they say, He became the Son, and that He was not the Son before this, but merely the Logos" (4th Oration). All of this is the direct continuation of the philosophy of the Hermetic writings.

In the latest version of the so-called Athanasian Creed, recently issued by the archiepiscopal committee, the old Egyptian distinction is expressed almost in the old words, "begotten before all time," and "born in time." The distinction of eternity before time, which the West could hardly grasp or feel to be of any importance, has been fastened by the two Egyptian presbyters upon all later Christianity.

FIG. 52.—Pottery figure of Isis and Horus, as a girl with an infant. Painted with red and blue stripes.

72. *The Madonna and the Bambino.*

As in practice and in dogma, so also in adoration, Egypt has dominated over Christianity. The devotion to the Virgin is unmistakably a late development of belief. Not a single festival of the Virgin, or a single dogma about her, appears for the first five centuries; but from that point onward there has been a steady flow of new customs and beliefs down to our own times, when in 1854 the Immaculate Conception and perfect sinlessness of the Virgin became an article of faith necessary to Salvation in the Roman Church.

In the earlier ages the first figure of Mary enthroned is of the date 540, at Parenzo. The earliest certain figures are in historic scenes of 433. The gilded glass figures, without nimbus, associated in equality with other saints, probably date from 300 to 400. There are also some fresco figures without names or any attributes which have been supposed to represent Mary, but without any ground for such a decision. There seems no question that Mary was regarded like any other saint of important position, down to the time of the condemnation of the Nestorian heresy in 431; after that date can be seen a steady growth of regard, adoration, and finally dogmatic compulsion.

None of the earlier figures represent Mary with her Son. The sharp transition from the types of the Good Shepherd, the Worker of miracles, and the Man of Sorrows, as shown in the earlier paintings, to the type of the Infant, is one of the strangest changes of conception in Christian Art. Such an entire reversal of idea could not be overlooked by a devout student such as Mrs. Jameson, who in her *Legends of the Madonna*, regards Cyril of Alexandria (about 430) as having probably brought in the type from his familiarity with Isis and Horus in Egypt.

There is, however, no need to look to Cyril for this change. Isis with Horus, the Queen of Heaven, the mother of God, the patroness of sailors, had already for some centuries been the greatest divinity of the civilised world. In the second century B.C. the temples of Isis at Puteoli and Pompeii were set up, with their ritual, priesthood, and worshippers spreading the foreign cult. By 80 B.C. even the conservative leader Sulla had to tolerate the Isiac guild of shrine bearers established in Rome itself. In a reaction of the government in 50 B.C. not a single workman would touch the shrine of Isis when ordered to destroy it. By 43 B.C. the sight of the priests of Isis was so usual, that a political refugee could escape in that disguise; and the next year the Triumvirs officially built a temple of Isis, and so adopted her in the Roman State. A century later in 69 A.D. the Emperor himself, clad as a priest of Isis, publicly sacrificed to the great goddess. In the same year Domitian escaped in the civil war as a priest of Isis, and later he rebuilt her temple in splendour; in the following century her position remained unchallenged.

Where Rome conquered, Isis was honoured. Her altars are found far west in Spain and at York; in the northern bounds of Holland, Switzerland, and the German baths; in the southern lands of Algier, and scattered in the intervening countries. Her

FIG. 53.—Pottery figure of Isis and Horus, with drapery over the head.

To face page 138.

worship was spread so that, even in the first century, Lucan called her the deity of the nations.

What was this worship which thus captivated the Roman world? The great picture of it is in the eleventh book of the *Lucius* of Apuleius, the sanctified end to that orgy of romance. The brilliant procession of devotees and priests, carrying sacred objects and shrines, is described. The consecrated priests were entirely devoted to the worship, clad in garments of white linen, drawn close over the breast, and hanging down to the feet. They took a new name in religion, and were subject to various kinds of abstinence. Two daily services of complicated ritual were their perpetual duty; and they stood as mediators to mankind, to prepare souls for a higher life.

The devotion of Lucius gives a reflection of the deep feelings which this worship brought forth. He adores Isis: "Interrupting my words with frequent sobs, and, as it were, half swallowing my voice, I thus addressed her, 'Thou, O holy and perpetual preserver of the human race, always munificent in cherishing mortals, dost bestow the sweet affection of a mother on the misfortunes of the wretched. Nor is there any day or night, nor so much as the minutest particle of time, which passes unattended by thy bounties. Thou dost protect man both by sea and land, and, dispersing the storms of life, dost extend thy health-giving right hand, by which thou dost . . . restrain the malignant influences of the stars. . . . The stars move responsive to thy command, the gods rejoice in thy divinity, the seasons return by thy appointment, and the elements are thy servants.

... But I ... have far from eloquence sufficient to express all that I conceive of thy majesty; not a thousand mouths, and tongues as many, not an eternal flow of unwearied speech, would be equal to the task.'"

The most popular form of Isis in the later centuries, just before the appearance of the Madonna and Bambino in Christian Art, was that of Isis the Mother nursing Horus the Child. In the illustrations here are some of the later Egyptian figures. Any of them might be supposed to be an Italian Madonna; and the latest of them is strikingly like the bronze work of the seventh or eighth century. Yet this latest shows the girdle tie of Isis, the lock of hair on Horus, and remains of the crowns, which stamp it as unquestionably a Pagan figure (Figs. 52, 53, 54).

Thus we see that there had been growing for many centuries an ardent devotion to the Queen of Heaven, the Mother of God, the Patroness of sailors, in Italy, and thence over all the Roman world. In the third and fourth centuries this worship was specially directed to the type of the mother and son. Then in the fifth century the names utterly disappear; and immediately there appears devotion hitherto entirely unknown in Christianity, a devotion to precisely the same figures with the same attributes, but with other names. The transformation is unmistakable. The new importation into Christianity was Isis and Horus, whose names alone had been banished.

If, now, we try our historical imagination by supposing that there had never been any of the refinements of the Trinitarian controversy, that no

FIG. 54.—Pottery figure of Isis and Horus, with the girdle tie of Isis and the crown, lock of hair, and round vase of Horus; these prove that this is an entirely pagan figure, though probably of the fourth or fifth century A.D., and show how completely this type was established before being appropriated to the Madonna.

To face page 140.

monastery had ever sterilised the best of the race, and that the Madonna and Bambino were alike unknown to devotion and to art, we may gain some sense of what changes Egypt wrought in Christianity, and how utterly foreign to the Judaic origin was its influence. But for Egypt, it is certain that the Goth would have continued the ancient civilisation of the world in Spain and Italy, which were lost owing to the bitter separation of the Athanasian struggle. But for Egypt, there would have been no force in the monotheism of Islam, which gave the power of bigotry to the Arab hordes, who resented the epithet "Mother of God" as blasphemy. It is the irony of every religion that the most popular parts of it are those which do not belong to it, but which have been brought into it from those beliefs which it tried to supersede. Islam had to accept the idolatry to a black stone, the pilgrimage in its honour, the worship of local saints—all quite antagonistic to its principles, and yet proving to be the favourite customs of its professed followers. So Christianity had thrust on it the system of seclusion, the pagan metaphysics about eternity and time and Divine emanations, and the devotion to the Mother and Child—all antagonistic to its original form, and yet proving to be the most prominent features of its general acceptance. It is from Egypt that each of these transformations has arisen, which paganised the original teaching of the renovated and spiritualised Israel. Egypt and Israel represent an antagonism which is at the very foundations of all religious thought, and which has lasted for four thousand years down to our own age.

DETAILED WORKS ON THE FOREGOING SUBJECTS.

CHAPTER
I. "Hyksos and Israelite Cities," W. M. F. PETRIE. 1906.
II. "Pithom," Dr. E. NAVILLE. £1.
"Hyksos and Israelite Cities." 1906. £1 1s.
III. "Researches in Sinai," W. M. F. PETRIE. 1906. £1.
V. "La liste de Sheshonq à Karnak," G. MASPERO (Victoria Institute Journal, 1890).
"Student's History of Egypt, III," W. M. F. PETRIE. 1905. 6s.
VI. "Tanis II," W. M. F. PETRIE. 1888. £1.
"The Aswan Papyri," A. H. SAYCE and A. COWLEY; and "Revue Archéologique," x. 432. £2 2s.
VII. "Hyksos and Israelite Cities." 1906. £1. 1s.
VIII. "Personal Religion in Egypt before Christianity," W. M. F. PETRIE. 1909. 2s. 6d.
IX. "The Growth of the Gospels," W. M. F. PETRIE. 1910. 2s. 6d.
X. "The Agapé and the Eucharist," Dr. J. F. KEATING. 1901. 4s. 6d.
"The Oxyrhynchus Papyri," B. P. GRENFELL and A. S. HUNT. 1898. (i. 177.) £1.
"Personal Religion in Egypt," W. M. F. PETRIE. 1909.
"The Orations of Athanasius against the Arians."
"Roman Society from Nero to Aurelius," Sir SAMUEL DILL. 1905. 15s.
APULEIUS, "Metamorphoses," xi.

INDEX

AAHMES, king, 50, 92-93
Aaron's rod, 62
Abijah, king, 68
Abimelech of Gerar, 21, 23
Abiyah, prophet, 71
Ablutions part of worship, 48
Abram, living at Beersheba, 24
　　　at Shechem, 70
　　migrations of, 20, 23
　　period of, 17, 37
Abram a brickmaker, 107
Ahrek, meaning of, 27
Absha, prince of the deserts, 13
Agapé, sources of, 131-132
Ahikam son of Shaphan, 90
Alaf, meaning of, 43
Amenhotep IV., king, 50
Ammon, kings descended from, 113
Amon, king, 88
Amorites in Syria, 15
　　mixed with Jews, 83
Amraphael, King of Shinar, 17
Ant-her, Hyksos king, 15
Antiochos Epiphanes, 98
Antonia, Castle of, 109
Apocrypha, 119
Apollos, 123
Apries (Hophra), king, 88, 92-93
Arab troops of Roman age, 14
Aramaic papyri of Aswan, 93-96
Arius, teaching of, 136
Ark and cherubim, 61
Asa, king, 68, 74, 75, 77

Asceticism foreign to the West, 133
Ashdod, 78
Asher, 25
Ashkelon, 78
Asklepios, definitions of, 112
Asshur-bani-pal, 86
Aswan, Jews at, 93-96
　　papyri from, 93-96
Athanasian Creed, 136

BAAL-ZEPHON, 39, 40
Babylonian kings of Egypt, 12, 13
Babylonianizing party, 90
Baptism an emblem, 117
Baruch, 90
Bathsheba, 68
Bedawyn life, 18, 22, 30
Beer-lahai-roi, 18, 24
Beersheba, Abram at, 24
Bells and pomegranates, 61, 62
Bethel stones, dreaming at, 49
Bezetha quarter, 109
Birth-rate, 58
Birth, simile of, 117
Bismarck, 68
Brazen sea, 48
Brickmaking in Egypt, 31-33, 107
Buddhist source of asceticism, 133
Burnt-offering on high place, 47

CALF, golden, 72
Camp of Hyksos, 18, 19
Canaanites mixed with Jews, 83

K

INDEX

Captivities, three, 81
Captivity, only a minority in, 82
Cave shrine, 47
Census lists of Israel, 42-46, 57-60
Cherubic figures, 61
Chieftainess of tribe, 21-26
Christianity a sect of Judaism, 130
Church ales, 132
Church of the Gentiles, 130
   of the Jews, 130
Circumcision, Egyptian, 21
   a tribal mark, 25
Cities in Syria, 51, 52
Civilisations, decay of, 11
Conical stones, 48
Constantine on Time and Eternity, 135
Conversion, types of, 116, 117
Coptic property held by women, 23
Copying of lists of conquests, 77
Creation by the Godhead, 113
   by the Logos, 115
Cushim troops, 72, 75
Cyrene, Persian conquest of, 112

DAPHNAE. *See* Tehaphnehes
David, 64, 65, 68
Deborah a mother in Israel, 26
Dinah, female judge, 24, 25
   Hivite alliance of, 25
Dionysiac festival, Jewish, 98
Divorce at Aswan, 94
Dowry at Aswan, 94
Dreamers in Sinai and at Jerusalem, 49

EDOM, coinage of, 22
Egypt and Israel, antagonism of, 141
   the ages of, 11
   Babylonian kings in, 12, 13
   famines in, 27
   influences on Israel, 60-63

Egyptian feasts in temples, 132
Elim, 40
Ephraim the centre of Israel, 71
Esarhaddon, 86
Essenes, 116, 134
Eternity, greater than Time, 135
   name of, 135
Etham, 39, 40
Ethiopian kingdom, 75, 86
Euphrates, Egyptian on the, 79
Exodus, character of Book of, 28
   date of, 37, 53
   numbers of, 40-46
   route of, 39
Ezekiel, holy city of, 70
   prophecies of, 80, 81, 83, 85

FAMINES, cause of migrations, 26
   in Egypt, 27
Feasts, at funerals, 131, 133
   in churches, 131, 132
Fire choked in foundations, 106
First-born, dedication of, 46
   numbers of, 41

GAZA, 77, 78, 86
Gedaliah, 82, 84, 85, 91
Genealogies of priesthood, 55-57
Genesis, civilisation in, 17
   contrasted with Exodus, 28
Genubath, prince, 65, 68
Gerer, belonged to Egyptians, 75, 78
   Phichol of, 21
   Sarah and Rebekah at, 23, 24
Gezer, expulsion of Canaanites from, 67
   population of, 30, 41
God, the Second, 114-115
Godhead, beliefs on the, 113-114
Goshen, settlement in, 28
Gospels, compilation of 125-126
   growth of, 127-129
   nucleus of, 126-127

INDEX

Greek mercenaries, 87
Greeks, dislike to, 112
    expelled from Egypt, 93
    in Daphnae, 87-89
    living with Jews, 88

HADAD, King of Edom, 64, 65, 68
Hagar an Egyptian, 20
Hagarenes, 21
Hammurabi, 17
Hand-maid substitute for mistress, 25
Hanun of Gaza, 77
Haran, 16
Hellenization of Jews, 97-98
Hermetic books, date of, 112-113
    on the Godhead, 113-114
    on the Logos, 114-116
    on conversion, 116-117
    linked to Christianity, 117-118
Hermetic philosophy continued by Arius, 136
Herod, building of, 105, 109
Hezekiah, 77
Hittites mixed with Jews, 83
Hophra, king, 88, 92-93
Hyksos, civilisation, 18
    fighting of, 20
    fortress, 18, 19
    invasion by, 11, 14, 15
    later movement of, 17
    migrations of, 26

IMAGES made by Israelites, 60, 61
Imhotep in Hermetic books, 112
Immaculate conception, dogma of, 137
Incense offering on altar, 48
Indian source of asceticism, 133
    theosophy, 117
Indians, named in Perfect Sermon, 113
    in Greece and Egypt, 134

Isaac, marriage of, 24
Ishmael half Egyptian, 20
    marries an Egyptian, 21
Isis, prototype of the Madonna, 138-140
    worship of, 138-139
Israelites, incorporate other peoples, 57-60
    influenced by Egypt, 60-63
    life in Egypt, 30-36
    not all in Egypt, 34
    numbers of, at Exodus, 41-46
    in Canaan, 57-60
    organisation, 31
    view of Jerusalem, 70

JACOB, at Mamre, 18
    at Shechem, 70
    blessing of, 47
Jacob-el, name in Syria, 34
Jehoahaz, 79
Jehoiakim, 79, 88
Jeremiah, prophecies of, 90-92
Jerusalem, new, in Egypt, 108-110
    not the city of Israel, 71
Jeshua, high priest, 98
Johanan, 84, 89
John, Gospel of St., 116
Joseph, period of, 27
Joseph-el, name in Syria, 35
Josephus, on Hyksos, 14
    on Oniah, 100, 108
Joshua, early date of parts in, 67
Josiah, 78, 88
Judas Maccabaeus, 99
Judges, history of, 54-56

KARAMAT, queen, 68, 69, 75
Karnak sculpture of Shishak, 73
Khammurabi. *See* Hammurabi
Khendy, King of Egypt and Babylonia, 12

INDEX

Khenzer, Babylonian King of Egypt, 13
Khyan, King of the Hyksos, 14, 15
Korē Kosmou, 112, 116, 135

LACHISH, plan of, 52
"Law of Piety," 134
Leah, tribal head, married first, 24
Levites, history of the, 46
Logia, value of, 124-125
Logos, growth of doctrine of the, 114-116
Longevity of patriarchs, 16
Lotus border, 62
Love-feasts, 131-133
Lubim troops, 72, 75
Luke, Gospel of St., 127-128
Lunar kalendar followed under Solomon, 66

MAAT, goddess of truth, 61
Madonna, adoration of, 137-141
Mamre, 18, 24
Manasseh, 87
Manetho, on Hyksos, 14, 20
Marah, 40
Mark, Gospel of St., 127-128
Mary, figures of, 137
Matthew, 125
    Gospel of St., 127-128
Menelaos, high priest, 98
Mercy and Truth, 61
Merenptah, king, 35, Fig. 26, 50
Mesopotamian rulers of Egypt, 12, 13
Metal vases of Syria, 50
Midwives, number of, 46
Migdol, 39
Migration of Semites, 15, 16, 17, 20, 23
    caused by drought and famine, 26, 27
Miriam, 25

Monasticism, Buddhist, 133
    pagan, 133
    rise of, 133-134
Morality, standards of, 22
Moses judged all disputes, 46
Mother in Israel, 25, 26
    of the tribe, 21-26
Muqayyer, 16
Musical instruments, 88
Muzri, kingdom of, 76

NAAMAH, 68, 72
Nabathaean coinage, 22
Nabopolassar, era of, 81
Nebuchadrezzar, 79, 80, 81, 92-93
Necho, 78, 79
Nectanebo, 113
New Jerusalem of Oniah, 108-110
Nile, statue of the, 75
No, city of, 85
Nomad civilisation, nature of, 17, 30
Noph, 85
Norse festivals in temples, 132
Nucleus of the Gospels, 126-127
Numbers of Israelites at Exodus, 41-46
    in Canaan, 57-60

OATHS by strange gods, 95, 96
Odeynat of Palmyra, 23
Omer, measure, 62
Oniah III., high priest, 98
Oniah IV., history of, 98-99
    land of, 97
    new Jerusalem of, 108-110
    petition of, 100
    temple of, 101-105
Organization of Israelites, 31
Oxyrhynchus, 124

PACHOMIOS, first Christian monk, 133

INDEX 149

Palmyra, Queen of, 23
Pankhy, king, 75
Parenzo, 137
Pasebkhanu, king, 65, 67, 68, 75
Passover, of Oniah, 106
    ovens, 105
Pathros, 85
Patriarchs, migrations of, 16, 17, 18
Pauline use of Book of Wisdom, 118-123
Pavement of Tehaphnehes, 92
Perfect Sermon, of Persian age, 113, 116, 135
Persian allusions in Hermetic books, 112-113
Pharaoh's daughter, 66
Phichol an Egyptian name, 21
Philo, 96, 114
Pihahiroth, 39
Pithom, city of, 33, 39
Plagues on Egypt, 35
Polygamy, political value of, 66
Population of Palestine, numbers of, 60, 82-84
Pot of manna, 62
Priesthood, genealogies of, 55-57
Prince of the desert, title, 13, 15, 20
Property, descent of, in Egypt, 23
Psamtek I., 78, 87
Psamtek II., 80

RABSHAKEH, 77
Rameses II., 33, Fig. 25, 50
Rameses III., 51
Rameses, city of, 33, 36
Ray of light an emblem, 116
Rebekah independent of Isaac, 24
Rebirth, simile of, 117
Rehoboam, 68, 71, 73
Rephidim, 40

SARAH, the chieftainess, 23
Sargon in Palestine, 77, 82, 86

Satrap named in *Korē Kosmou*, 112
Saul, reign of, 53
Scythian invasion, 78
    named in Perfect Sermon, 113
Secret Sermon, 117
Semites mixing with Egyptians, 14, 20, 21
    movements of, 15, 16, 17
Semqen, Hyksos king, 15
Serabīt, temple at, 47-49
    worship at, 48
    writing at, 31, 32
Serah, 25
Sermon on the Mount, 128
Sety I., king, 50
Shabaka, king, 75, 76, 86
Shabatoka, king, 77
Sharuhen, 50
Shechem, 17
    the old centre, 70, 71, 72
"Shepherd of Men," 115
Sheshenq. *See* Shishak
Shiloh, 70, 71
Shishak, 51, 65, 68, 71
    invasion by, 72-74
Shrine in a cave, 47
Siamen, king, 65
Sibe of Muzri, 77
Sinai, Semitic life in, 22
Sleeping-places for dreaming, 49
So, king, 76
Stairways of Oniah, 103-104
Standards of weight and measure, 62
Stone building of Herod and Oniah, 105
Store cities, 33
Straw for brickmaking, 33
Sua, king, 76
Succoth, land of, 34, 39, 73
Suez, Gulf of, 39
Sukkim troops, 72
Sumerians, 15
Syene. *See* Aswan

INDEX

Syria subject to Egypt, 50
Syrian cities, 51, 52
Syro-Mesopotamian mercenaries, 12

TABLES of the Law, 62
Taharqa. *See* Tirhakah
Tahpanhes. *See* Tehaphnehes
Tahpenes, queen, 65, 68
Tahutmes I., conquest by, 50
Tahutmes III., conquest by, 50
Tanis, kings of, 64
Tartan, viceroy, 76
Tehaphnehes, a fortress, 85, 87
    Greeks in, 87–89
    pavement at, 92–93
    social importance of, 87
Tell-el-Hesy, 19
Tell-el-Yehudiyeh, 18, 102
Temple of Jerusalem, 98
    of Oniah, 101–105
    of Serabīt, 47–49
    of Yahu, 94, 96
    of Zerubbabel, 103
Terah, migration of, 16
Therapeutae, feasts of, 132
Three days' journey in the wilderness, 40
Tiglath Pileser III., 86
Time different from Eternity, 135
    Egyptian name of, 135
Tirhakah, 77, 86
Tribal Mother, 21–26
Tribes, census of the, 42–46, 57–60
Trinitarian controversy, 136, 140
Truth, figures of, 61

Turanians in Babylonia, 15
Turquoise mining, 47

UNIVERSAL Mind, treatise on the, 113
Ur, migration from, 16
Usarkon, 68, 74

VICEROYS of Ethiopia, 75, 77
Virgin, adoration of, 137–141

WADY Gharandel, 40
Wady Hawara, 40
Wahaballat of Palmyra, 23
Way, the doctrine of the, 130
Weights and measures protected in temples, 62
Wisdom, Book of, known to Paul, 119–123
    personification of, 119
Women, independent position of, 21–26
Writing, common use of, 125

YEHUDIYEH, Tell el, 18, 102
Yule feast, 132

ZEDEKIAH, 80, 88, 91
Zerah, king, 74, 77
Zerubbabel, temple of, 103
Zeynab, Zenobia, 23
Zilpah, 25
Zoan, city of, 85
    kings of, 64

www.ingramcontent.com/pod-product-compliance
Lightning Source LLC
Chambersburg PA
CBHW040259170426
43193CB00020B/2944